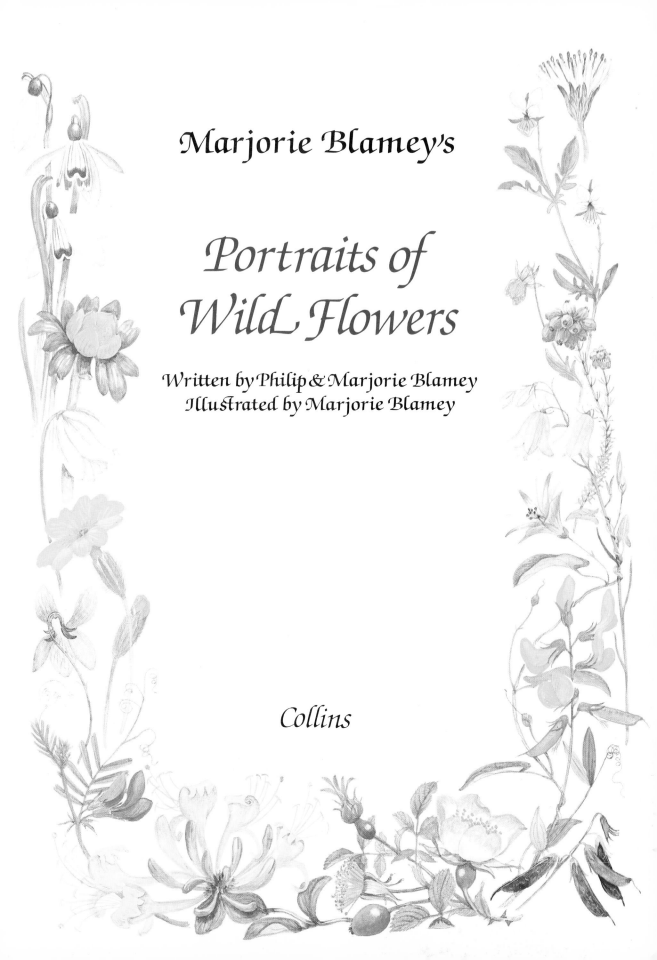

Marjorie Blamey's

Portraits of Wild Flowers

Written by Philip & Marjorie Blamey
Illustrated by Marjorie Blamey

Collins

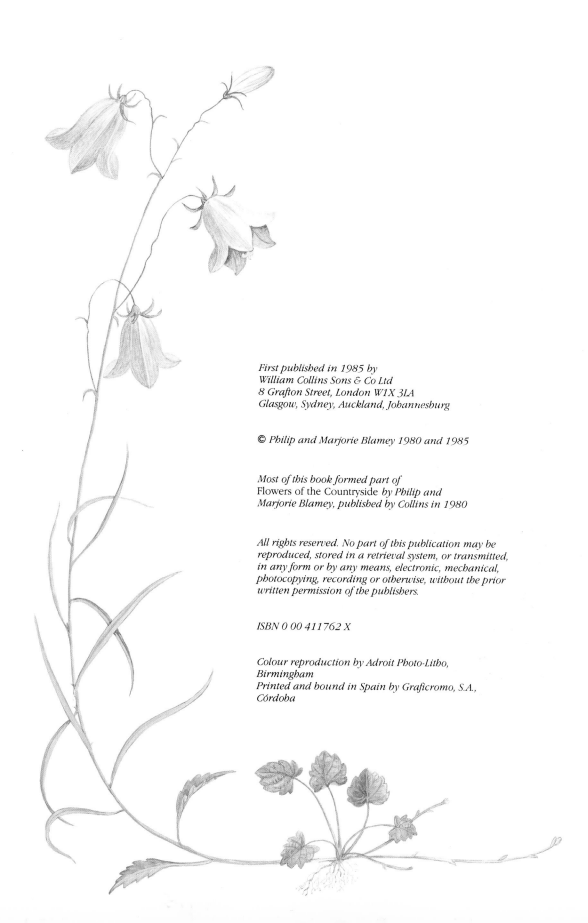

First published in 1985 by
William Collins Sons & Co Ltd
8 Grafton Street, London W1X 3LA
Glasgow, Sydney, Auckland, Johannesburg

© *Philip and Marjorie Blamey 1980 and 1985*

Most of this book formed part of
Flowers of the Countryside *by Philip and*
Marjorie Blamey, published by Collins in 1980

ISBN 0 00 411762 X

Colour reproduction by Adroit Photo-Litho,
Birmingham
Printed and bound in Spain by Graficromo, S.A.,
Córdoba

Introduction

I was asked to choose all the flowers I
particularly liked and to paint their portraits
for this book. I thought of all the wonderful
flowers we had seen on our travels because
at that time I could have chosen any
countryside. I could have chosen the brilliant
Flame Trees of Africa, for example, or the
lovely Frangipanis with their heavenly scent,
the Jacarandas, Morning Glories or
Oleanders, flowers whose very names
conjure up the heat and sunshine of the Far
East. However, after much thought I finally
chose the wild flowers of our own
countryside, which though smaller and paler
in comparison with the exotic blooms of far
away, have such charm and fragile beauty, so
much variety of colour and shape that I find
them not only irresistible, but also
increasingly important additions to the
quality of my life. A world without flowers
would be dull indeed. The more I see of the
splendours of the flowers of other parts of

Coltsfoot and daisies

the world, the more I value our own flora and it is always a joy to return home to the cool, clear beauty of a simple primrose.

I have feelings of rage and despair though at the careless or deliberate destruction of our wild flowers and their habitats. So many are exterminated in the arable fields of the corn-growing areas where no hedges are left for them to hide in. No poppy must stain the golden miles of corn, nor buttercup mark the monoculture of the grasslands. It is with mixed feelings of pleasure, sadness and envy that we see the colourful meadows of France and other European countries where all our banished flowers flourish abundantly. These sweet-smelling 'weeds' provide mineral-rich hay which is sufficient for smaller European herds of cows, whereas in Britain our intensive system of dairy farming demands more and more fields to grow food for cattle until we have run out of countryside for wild flowers to flourish in.

Our traditional meadows with their unique flora — Green-winged Orchids and Adderstongues, Cowslips, Salad Burnet and Scabious — are now few and far between, although many are protected areas. The modern farmer values them little because he only wants the heavily fertilized and sprayed crop of grass produced by monoculture. He ploughs up these old fields his forebears so carefully nurtured over the centuries and destroys the hedgerows in which any remaining plant may survive. We are losing many ancient acres and their equally valuable and ancient flora in this way and once gone they can never be re-created.

These are some of the reasons which compel me to seek out and paint our wild flowers over and over again. Soon many of them will survive only in fields, woodlands and marshes which are owned and managed by conservation trusts. I feel that a lifetime is not long enough to appreciate their delights fully, to marvel at nature's resemblance of the Bee Orchid to its namesake, or to

Field Bindweed

unpack the bud of a scarlet poppy from its green suitcase and watch its creased petals ironed out by the sun and wind. Merely to hold a wild flower − it doesn't matter which one − and to try to appreciate its beauty is important to me, for next year it may have disappeared, been sprayed with herbicide, covered with concrete or ploughed out of existence. I often fear that I may be painting a rare flower growing in our countryside for the last time. I may still be able to paint it in other parts of Europe but it will not be with the same feeling of pleasure and pride.

Many plants have interesting and ancient names and their history of medical and culinary uses makes them fascinating subjects to research. Painting their portraits became a full-time occupation so I was fortunate to be able to pass over the work of writing about them to my husband, Philip, who shares my enthusiasm and concern about the future of the wild flowers of our countryside.

The illustrations in this book have been reproduced from watercolour paintings. Watercolour is the medium I prefer for depicting small and detailed flower subjects. The flowers we have chosen for this book follow the order of classification of the two Collins field guides I illustrated, *The Wild Flowers of Britain and Northern Europe* and *The Alpine Flowers of Britain and Europe*. These field guides include detailed identification texts on all the flowers illustrated here and many more species than we have room for in this book.

Water-pepper

Persicaria

Male flowers

Hop

Pellitory
of the Wall

Mature hops

Knotgrass

The Hemp, Nettle, Dock, Purslane and Goosefoot families

Found in hedges and damp woodland, **Hop** *(Humulus lupulus)* grows by twining up its supports in a clockwise direction. The female flowers, used to flavour beer, appear from July to September. The male flowers bloom at the same time on separate plants. The Hop has been cultivated since the 9th century when it was introduced from Holland. It is a member of the Hemp family (Cannabaceae) whose only other representative in Britain is *Cannabis sativa,* also known as Hemp, which was grown in great quantities in the 18th and 19th centuries for its fibre.

Pellitory of the Wall *(Parietaria judaica)*, as its name implies, grows in walls and rocky banks in western Europe. The insignificant flowers appear from June to October on reddish stems. In medieval times it was used medicinally, as were other members of the Nettle family (Urticaceae).

Persicaria *(Polygonum persicaria)* is one of the first weeds to colonize newly reclaimed lowlands. It is a member of the Dock family (Polygonaceae). Known also as Redshank, it flowers from June to October. The black blotches on the leaves are said to be the marks of the blood of Christ, or alternatively, the fingermarks of the Devil when he cast it aside as Useless (yet another name) because he mistook it for **Water-pepper** *(P. hydropiper)*. This plant grows in damp meadows, wet mud and shallow water, flowering from July to September. It has a peppery taste and care should be taken not to touch the eyes after handling it. **Knotgrass** *(P. aviculare)* sprawls on bare ground and seashores and flowers from June to September. William Turner called it 'Swyne gyrs' because it was fed to pigs to improve their appetite.

Fairly recent newcomers to Europe are the two purslanes (Portulacaceae). **Pink Purslane** *(Montia sibirica)* was first recorded in 1838 in damp woodlands and on stream banks. It flowers from April to July, as does its relative **Spring Beauty** *(M. perfoliata)*, also known as the Buttonhole Flower and first found in 1837. Its flowers are supported by the leaves which completely surround the stem. It grows on light acid soil.

In spite of both its names, **Sea Purslane** *(Halimione portulacoides)* is in fact a member of the Goosefoot family (Chenopodiaceae). A halophyte, it grows within the tidal reaches of salt marshes.

Pink Purslane

Spring Beauty

Sea Purslane

7

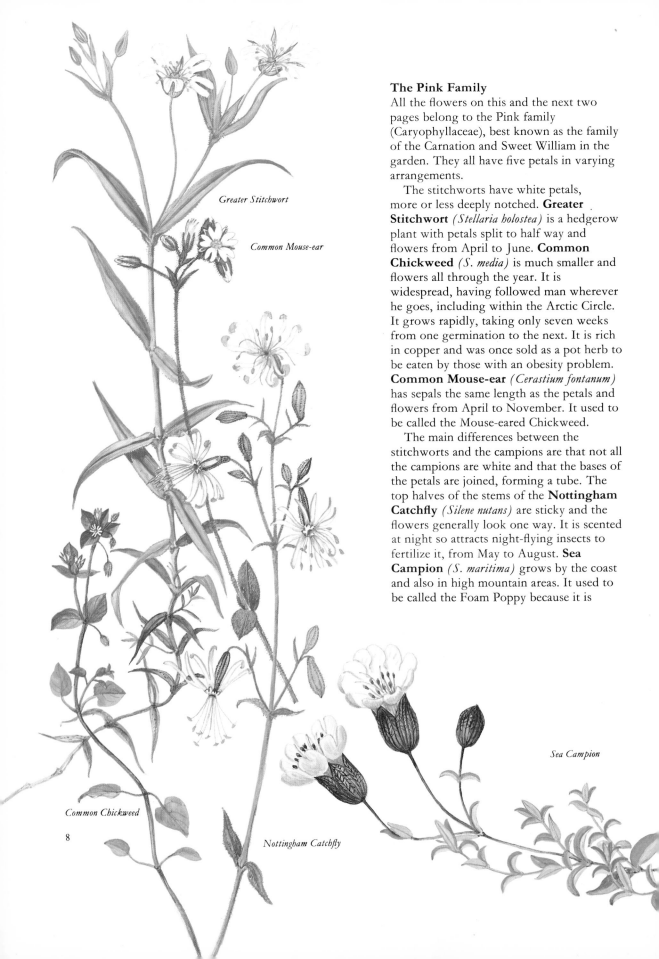

Greater Stitchwort

Common Mouse-ear

Common Chickweed

Nottingham Catchfly

Sea Campion

The Pink Family

All the flowers on this and the next two pages belong to the Pink family (Caryophyllaceae), best known as the family of the Carnation and Sweet William in the garden. They all have five petals in varying arrangements.

The stitchworts have white petals, more or less deeply notched. **Greater Stitchwort** *(Stellaria holostea)* is a hedgerow plant with petals split to half way and flowers from April to June. **Common Chickweed** *(S. media)* is much smaller and flowers all through the year. It is widespread, having followed man wherever he goes, including within the Arctic Circle. It grows rapidly, taking only seven weeks from one germination to the next. It is rich in copper and was once sold as a pot herb to be eaten by those with an obesity problem. **Common Mouse-ear** *(Cerastium fontanum)* has sepals the same length as the petals and flowers from April to November. It used to be called the Mouse-eared Chickweed.

The main differences between the stitchworts and the campions are that not all the campions are white and that the bases of the petals are joined, forming a tube. The top halves of the stems of the **Nottingham Catchfly** *(Silene nutans)* are sticky and the flowers generally look one way. It is scented at night so attracts night-flying insects to fertilize it, from May to August. **Sea Campion** *(S. maritima)* grows by the coast and also in high mountain areas. It used to be called the Foam Poppy because it is

favoured by insects of the family
Cercopidae, which are responsible for
producing cuckoo-spit. The grub lives
within the foam as protection against
predators. The plant flowers from May to
September, at the same time as **White
Campion** *(S. alba)* which is sweetly scented
at night thus attracting moths, especially the
Elephant Hawkmoth. Its seed capsule has
ten upright teeth, whereas **Red Campion**
(S. dioica) has teeth which are tightly rolled
back. These two plants hybridize in damp
hedges and woodlands to produce a pale-
pink form. The **Bladder Campion**
(S. vulgaris), so called after the inflated tube at
the base of the flower, prefers dry grassland.
It blooms from May to September,
producing a seed capsule with six teeth. In
contrast, the seed capsule of the **Soapwort**
(Saponaria officinalis) is a long thin tube,
giving the effect of the flowers growing on
stalks. It is generally a garden throw-out,
being invasive and obstinate, and flowers in
waste ground from June to September—a
month earlier than **Ragged Robin** *(Lychnis
floscuculi)* whose five petals are so deeply cut
that they appear to be ten in number. This
delightful plant is found in damp and
marshy ground.

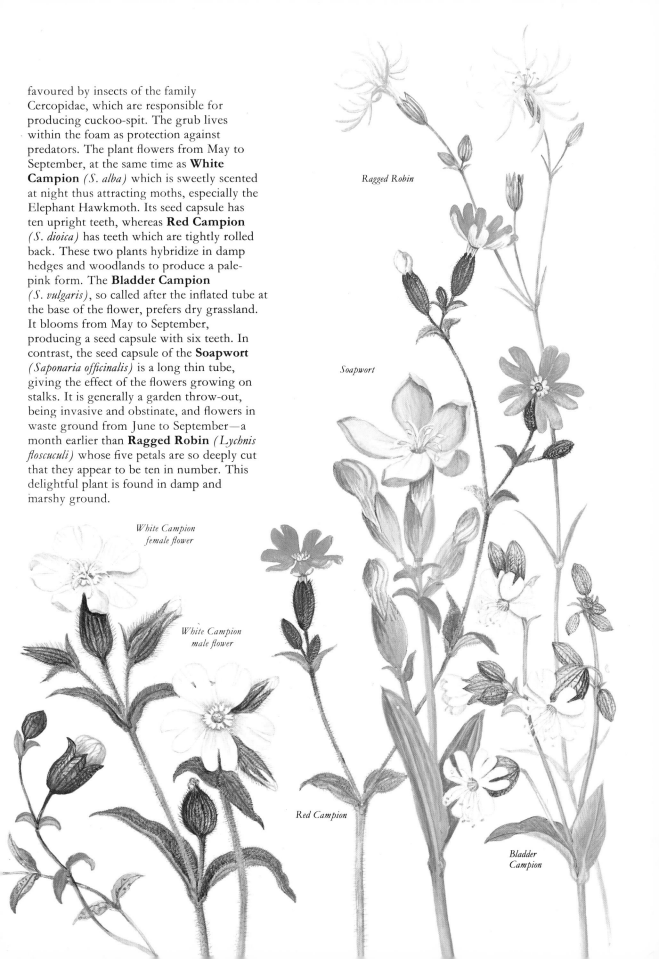

Ragged Robin

Soapwort

*White Campion
female flower*

*White Campion
male flower*

Red Campion

*Bladder
Campion*

Deptford Pink

Wild Pink

Clove Scented Pink

*Maiden
Pink*

The name Dianthus is said to be
derived from the ancient Greek
words for 'flower of the gods'—*Dios
anthos*—and we can see every
justification for it on this page.

Deptford Pink *(Dianthus armeria)*
is an annual whereas all the others are
perennial. It flowers from June to
August in dry sandy places and is a
rare native in Britain, unlike the
Wild Pink *(D. plumarius)* which may
be seen on the walls of old Norman
Castles, confirming the suggestion
that it was introduced to Britain when
the castles were built of imported
stone. In medieval times it was the
symbol of true love.

The **Clove Scented Pink**
(D. caryophyllus) is almost certainly
the 'gillyflower' of Shakespeare's time.
The name was anglicized from the
Old French *girofle* meaning 'love
flower'. Both Clove and Wild Pinks
are fragrant and were crossed and
bred to produce the highly scented
garden carnation.

Maiden Pink *(D. deltoides)* is not
fragrant. It was so named by John
Gerard in the 16th century because
he thought it was a 'virgin like
pinke' with a blush to match. All
these pinks flower from June to
August and grow best in a limey,
light soil.

The Buttercup and Water-lily families

Ponds and still waters may be covered with the round leaves of the **White Water-lily** *(Nymphaea alba)*, which appear to support the flower. It blooms from June to September. In Elizabethan times, those who wished to maintain their chastity would eat the seeds and dry powdered stem! **Yellow Water-lily** *(Nuphar lutea)* is said to smell of alcohol which accounts for one of its names, Brandy Bottle. The flowers do not float but are held several inches above the water on erect stems.

To eat any of the remaining plants on this page would be foolhardy since most of the Buttercup family (Ranunculaceae) are poisonous. **Stinking Hellebore** *(Helleborus foetidus)* grows on dry scrubland. The seeds are spread by snails which deposit them in their slime. The stems stand through the winter, unlike those of **Green Hellebore** *(H. viridis)* which flowers in damp places and woods and then withers away. It is rather rare, whereas **Winter Aconite** *(Eranthis hyemalis)* is more plentiful and one of the earliest harbingers of spring with its ruff of lobed leaves. Introduced from southern Europe about four hundred years ago, it is grown extensively in gardens.

Green Hellebore

Stinking Hellebore

Yellow Water-lily

White Water-lily

Winter Aconite

Globe Flower

Marsh Marigold

Lesser Spearwort

*Common
Water Crowfoot*

Globe Flower *(Trollius europaeus)* grows in damp pastures, often in mountains. We have seen and admired it growing amongst violas in high meadows in the Pyrenees. In the 16th century it was known by its old English name of 'locker gowan', meaning 'closed flower'. Far older than this though is the **Marsh Marigold** *(Caltha palustris)* which grew in Britain before the last Ice Age. Also known as Kingcup, it was cultivated by John Parkinson in his garden in the double form, but he left the single form to grow 'in its proper place', as he said. We have both forms by our pond.

Also to be found in or near water is **Lesser Spearwort** *(Ranunculus flammula)* which flowers from June to October and was used medicinally in the Middle Ages as a blistering agent, as many of this family were. It is native to Britain, as is **Common Water Crowfoot** *(R. aquatilis)* which grows in slow-moving water up to a depth of three feet. Its floating leaves are toothed, and those which are submerged are branched.

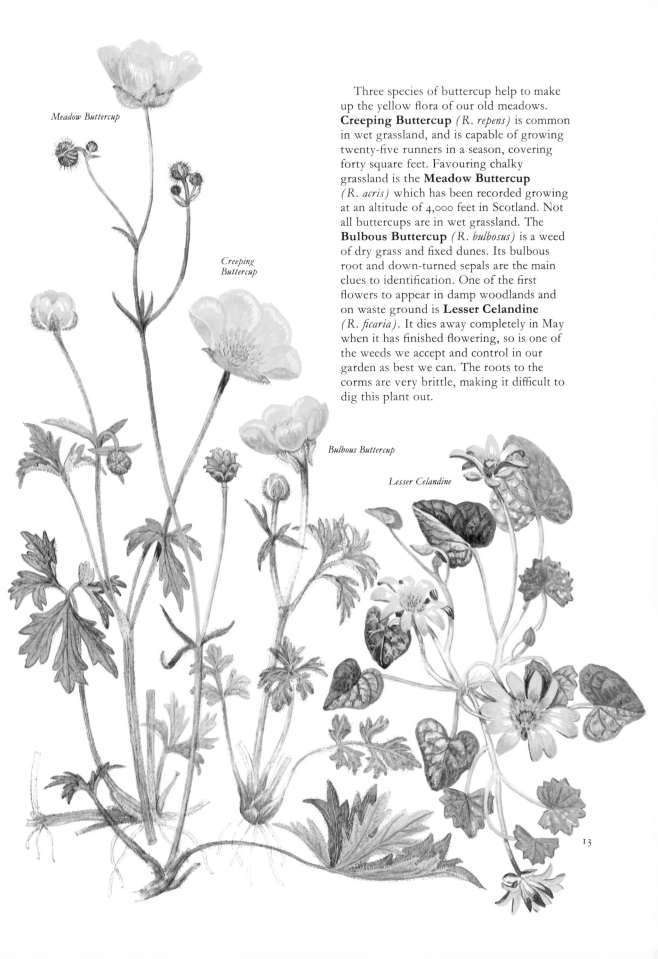

Meadow Buttercup

*Creeping
Buttercup*

Three species of buttercup help to make
up the yellow flora of our old meadows.
Creeping Buttercup *(R. repens)* is common
in wet grassland, and is capable of growing
twenty-five runners in a season, covering
forty square feet. Favouring chalky
grassland is the **Meadow Buttercup**
(R. acris) which has been recorded growing
at an altitude of 4,000 feet in Scotland. Not
all buttercups are in wet grassland. The
Bulbous Buttercup *(R. bulbosus)* is a weed
of dry grass and fixed dunes. Its bulbous
root and down-turned sepals are the main
clues to identification. One of the first
flowers to appear in damp woodlands and
on waste ground is **Lesser Celandine**
(R. ficaria). It dies away completely in May
when it has finished flowering, so is one of
the weeds we accept and control in our
garden as best we can. The roots to the
corms are very brittle, making it difficult to
dig this plant out.

Bulbous Buttercup

Lesser Celandine

13

Old Man's Beard

Columbine

Monkshood

Pasque Flower

Traveller's Joy

Wood Anemone

The plants illustrated here are those least like the usual image of flowers of the Buttercup family

Traveller's Joy *(Clematis vitalba)* was so called by John Gerard who found it growing beside the road when he was on his travels. Its flowers are small, fragrant and delicate and are seen from July to September. They are followed by the seed head which gives the plant its winter name of **Old Man's Beard**. In this form it can take over a hedge completely. Lengths of its stem used to be smoked by gypsies, and this is reflected in its vernacular names throughout Europe, like Gipsie's Bacca in Britain, *Bois à fumer* in France, *Smookhout* in Holland and *Rauchholz* in Germany.

Quite different is **Columbine** *(Aquilegia vulgaris)* which is often a garden escape. Both the English and scientific names refer to the birdlike qualities of the petals. *Aquila* is Latin for 'eagle' and refers to the claw-like spurs on the flowers, but more peaceful is the English name derived from the Latin word *columba* for 'doves'. The flower was said to resemble a group of five doves, and a glance at the illustration here shows why. Columbine blooms from May to July and is poisonous.

Also poisonous is **Monkshood** *(Aconitum napellus)*, the 'juice' from which was once used to poison the spears and other hunting weapons of the Greeks and Romans. A variant of Monkshood is Wolfsbane *(A. vulparia)*, so called because its poison was used in baiting wolf traps.

Pulsatillas and anemones have no petals but only brightly coloured sepals. The now rare **Pasque Flower** *(Pulsatilla vulgaris)* grows on dry grassy slopes and flowers from March to May. It has only one flower on each stem, like the **Wood Anemone** *(Anemone nemorosa)* which will grow in any but the most acid or waterlogged ground. Its natural habitat is deciduous woodland where it flowers from March to May.

Common Poppy

Welsh Poppy

Long-headed Poppy

Rough Poppy

Prickly Poppy

Common Fumitory

The Fumitory and Poppy families

A low-growing, straggling plant with smoke-blue foliage, **Common Fumitory** *(Fumaria officinalis)* was called in the Middle Ages *Fumus terrae,* 'smoke of the earth'—the smoke of the burning plant was said to cast out evil spirits. A weed of cultivated ground, it flowers from April to October. Its juice is an irritant, so care is needed after handling the plant.

In flamboyant contrast are the poppies. Ceres, the Roman goddess of agriculture, awoke so refreshed from a sleep induced by a poppy that she decreed that the poppy should always grow with corn, but seed-screening and spraying have put a stop to that. All poppies have four petals, some overlapping, others separate, like those of **Prickly Poppy** *(Papaver argemone)*, generally the first to flower in Britain, from May to July. The pod is long, narrow and bristly, while the much larger **Long-headed Poppy** *(P. dubium)* has a hairless pod and deeply overlapping petals when it flowers, from June to August. It is a plant of arable and disturbed ground as is the **Rough Poppy** *(P. hybridum)*. Rare in Britain, it blooms from June to August and has round pods with dense bristles. The **Common Poppy** *(P. rhoeas),* with a long hairless pod, is better known as the Flanders Poppy which grew profusely in the war zones of the First World War. It flowers from June to October. An edible oil is made from the seed and also one for mixing oil paints. Matthias de l'Obel, the Flemish botanist, found the **Welsh Poppy** *(Meconopsis cambrica)* growing in Wales in the 16th century. It flowers from June to August, producing a long, narrow pod, small when compared to that of the **Yellow Horned-poppy** *(Glaucium flavum)* which grows on shingle and coarse sand beaches along most European coastlines. The sap is orange and has an unpleasant smell. In medieval times it was used to reduce bruising.

Yellow Horned-poppy

17

Wild Cabbage

The Cabbage and Stonecrop families

The Cabbage family (Cruciferae) is one of the most important. Many vegetables are bred from wild species, as are several garden flowers. In sailing ships, the problem of scurvy used to be lessened by eating **Common Scurvy-grass** *(Cochlearia officinalis)* rich in vitamin C. A halophyte, it grows in salt marshes and also on shady cliffs where it is the first crucifer to bloom, in April.

Found at the back of beaches is **Sea Rocket** *(Cakile maritima)*. The flowers, seen from June to August, vary from white to pink. It tolerates shifting sand by growing long creeping roots which also help to stabilize the dunes. Different in habitat and habit of growth is **Hedge Mustard** *(Sisymbrium officinale)*, often flowering from May to September. Its spreading upper branches and seed pods close to the stem make it instantly recognizable.

Sprouts, cabbage, cauliflower and sprouting broccoli all come from the **Wild Cabbage** *(Brassica oleracea)* which grows on rocky cliffs in southern Britain and northern France and was first cultivated by the ancient Greeks.

Large Bittercress *(Cardamine amara)* flowers in

Hedge Mustard

Sea Rocket

Common Scurvy-grass

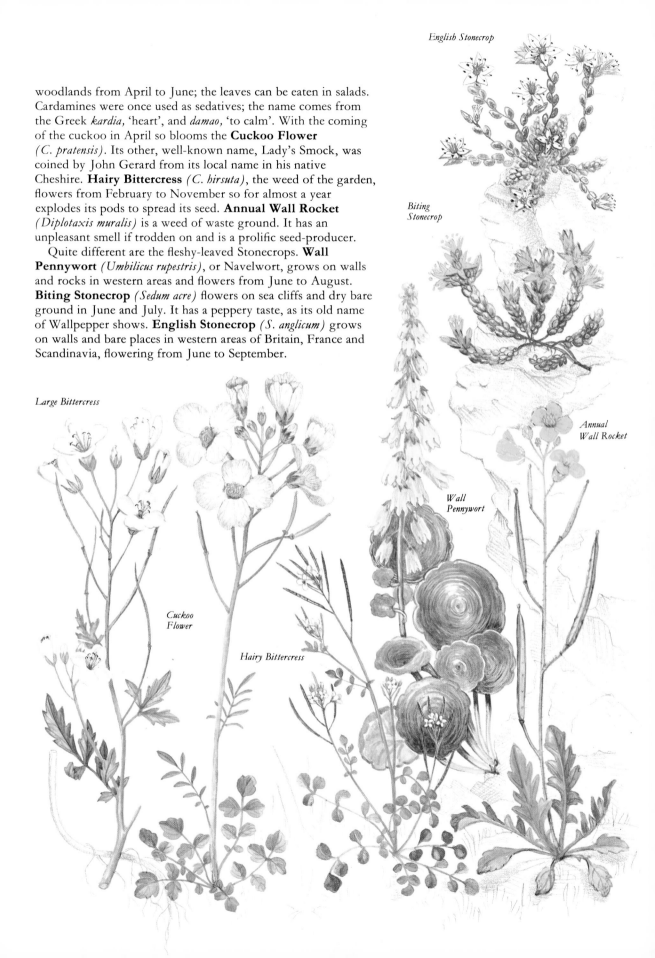

woodlands from April to June; the leaves can be eaten in salads. Cardamines were once used as sedatives; the name comes from the Greek *kardia,* 'heart', and *damao,* 'to calm'. With the coming of the cuckoo in April so blooms the **Cuckoo Flower** *(C. pratensis)*. Its other, well-known name, Lady's Smock, was coined by John Gerard from its local name in his native Cheshire. **Hairy Bittercress** *(C. hirsuta)*, the weed of the garden, flowers from February to November so for almost a year explodes its pods to spread its seed. **Annual Wall Rocket** *(Diplotaxis muralis)* is a weed of waste ground. It has an unpleasant smell if trodden on and is a prolific seed-producer.

Quite different are the fleshy-leaved Stonecrops. **Wall Pennywort** *(Umbilicus rupestris)*, or Navelwort, grows on walls and rocks in western areas and flowers from June to August. **Biting Stonecrop** *(Sedum acre)* flowers on sea cliffs and dry bare ground in June and July. It has a peppery taste, as its old name of Wallpepper shows. **English Stonecrop** *(S. anglicum)* grows on walls and bare places in western areas of Britain, France and Scandinavia, flowering from June to September.

English Stonecrop

Biting Stonecrop

Large Bittercress

Cuckoo Flower

Hairy Bittercress

Wall Pennywort

Annual Wall Rocket

Meadowsweet

Marsh Cinquefoil

Water Avens

Agrimony

Herb Bennet

The Rose family

On these pages are the first members of the Rose family to which belongs probably the best-known flower in the world. The family is very varied and includes many flowers unlike the rose itself.

The fragrance of **Meadowsweet** (*Filipendula ulmaria*) is one of the loveliest scents in the countryside in September. It grows, from two to four feet, in wet meadows, but this in fact has little to do with its name. It was once used for sweetening mead, or 'meodu' in Old English, and it is said that a pleasant drink can be made from the flowers. It was used as a strewing herb and as a decoration at weddings, hence the alternative name, Bridewort. It was used to cure malaria in the days when that scourge was rampant in Europe.

To cure snakebites and ease pain **Agrimony** (*Agrimonia eupatoria*) was recommended by both Dioscorides and Pliny. It grows in dry grassy places throughout Europe and on hedges and banks in limey areas. It has the smell of apricots and flowers from June to August.

The scientific name for **Herb Bennet** (*Geum urbanum*) shows it is scented, since *Geum* is a Latinized form of the Greek word *geuo,* 'agreeable flower'. The root is also scented and was used to freshen clothes cupboards and to repel moths. Legend has it that the powerful scent repelled the Devil, which led to its being hung up in houses for that very purpose, and it became known as the Blessed Herb or *Herba Benedicta*. It grows in dry woodland edges and occasionally hybridizes with its unlike cousin **Water Avens** (*G. rivale*)*,* producing extremely vigorous plants. Water Avens was first recorded in 1633 by Thomas Johnson, a London botanist and apothecary.

John Gerard found **Marsh Cinquefoil** (*Potentilla palustris*) growing near some ponds in the Colchester area and took some plants back to his garden where they 'flourish and prosper well', he said. They grow in wet limefree places.

'Cinquefoil' means literally 'five leaves' and Dioscorides called **Creeping Cinquefoil** *(P. reptans) Pentaphyllon* which was Latinized to *Potentilla,* also meaning 'five leaves'. It grows from a taproot of up to a foot in depth and spreads in damp shady places by means of runners. In sunny drier places, reproduction is by seed.

Tormentil *(P. erecta)* grows on acid heathland up to an altitude of 2,000 feet. In olden days colic was cured by drinking milk in which the roots of Tormentil had been boiled. In the Hebrides it was also used as a tanning agent for fishing nets.

The white flowers of the **Barren Strawberry** *(P. sterilis)* have led some people to confuse it with the **Wild Strawberry** *(Fragaria vesca),* but the petals of the former are notched while those of the latter are not. Although the latter is not the plant from which the large domestic strawberry was bred (its ancestors came from North America), the fruit is small and delicious. It grows in woods and hedgerows throughout Europe and flowers from April until June when the fruit is ready to eat.

Barren Strawberry

Wild Strawberry

Tormentil

Creeping Cinquefoil

Dog Rose

Roses are among the flowers longest favoured by man. The Ancient Greeks and Romans used the petals for perfume and even for carpeting. In the theory of signatures the thorn is said to resemble a dog's tooth, and, according to Pliny, a Roman soldier bitten by a mad dog applied the roots of a rose to the wound to cure it, hence the **Dog Rose** *(Rosa canina)* was credited with being a cure for hydrophobia. **Robin's Pincushion** is the gall or swelling often seen on the Dog Rose. It is caused by the Gall-wasp and is sometimes called a briar ball. Apothecaries used to powder them to make a drink to cure colic. The presence of the grub inside the gall was a bonus as it was dried, powdered and made into another drink which was used to 'drive forth the worms from the belly'.

The white **Field Rose** *(R. arvensis)* has been a favourite for hundreds of years. It grows in woods and hedges, is very fragrant and is the rose Shakespeare referred to as the Musk Rose.

The **Burnet Rose** *(R. pimpinellifolia)* is slightly fragrant and extremely spiny. It grows in dry open places, sometimes on sand dunes. It spreads quickly and is very difficult to eradicate from a garden, as we know. We have allowed it to stay but it is a constant struggle to keep it in the part of the garden allocated to it. **Sweet Briar** *(R. rubiginosa)* is sometimes called Eglantine. It grows in hedgerows and has scent glands on the back of the leaves so made a good strewing plant. **Downy Rose** *(R. tomentosa)* grows on hedges, generally in hilly districts. All the roses on these pages are native to Britain and are also generally found in Continental Europe except in the most northerly regions.

Field Rose

Burnet Rose

Downy Rose

Sweet Briar

Rosehips

Robin's Pincushion

23

Wild
Cherry

Hawthorn

Sloes

Blackthorn

Our last representatives of the Rose family are these three trees.
Hawthorn *(Crataegus monogyna)* is well known as a hedgerow
tree in Britain and is found throughout Continental Europe.
Because of its rapid growth as a hedging plant, it is also called
Quickthorn. The subject of many legends and much folklore—many
celebrations for the coming of summer are concerned with Hawthorn
(hence yet another name, May Tree)—it is said to be the tree from which
Christ's Crown of Thorns was made. Also according to legend, another
member of the same genus, the Glastonbury Thorn, sprang from the staff
of Joseph of Arimathea when he visited England after the Crucifixion.
Until fertilization the scent of the Hawthorn is unpleasant—said to be like
that of London during the plague—due to the presence of the chemical
trimethylamine whose smell of putrefaction attracts midges and flies.
After fertilization the scent changes to a very pleasant one.

    Blackthorn *(Prunus spinosa)* grows on scrubland throughout Europe.
It produces sloes as its fruit, from which is made that delicious liqueur
sloe gin. Its very hard wood is used for tool handles, and the famous Irish
shillelagh should be made of Blackthorn.

    In the 16th century, branches of **Wild Cherry** *(P. avium)* were sold,
complete with the fruit. It is little wonder, therefore, that the tree is not
as common as it was. As long ago as the time of Dioscorides, cherry
cough medicine was made from the gum which exudes from the wood.
The tree grows in hedges throughout Europe.

24

The Pea and Flax families

The Pea family (Leguminosae) is a valuable one economically since it includes vegetables and clover forage crops for grassland as well as ornamental flowers for the garden. **Spotted Medick** *(Medicago arabica)* grows in southern Britain and Continental Europe on grass verges. It is sometimes found on sandy ground near the sea. The black spots which distinguish it from other medicks are said, like the marks on Persicaria, to come from Christ's blood falling upon them at the foot of the Cross. The pods, curled into a spiral and with spines, contain the seeds which have a built-in capability of several years' dormancy.

Another plant with unusual pods is the **Horseshoe Vetch** *(Hippocrepis comosa)* whose name is a literal translation from Greek, describing the pod as a series of horseshoes linked together. It is deep-rooted and grows on chalky grassland. Birdsfoot Trefoil *(Lotus corniculatus)* has very straight narrow pods set at angles similar to those of the toes on a bird's foot. It is widespread in Europe.

Kidney Vetch *(Anthyllis vulneraria)* has yellow, orange, red, purple or white flowers, depending on its habitat. It grows at sea level, on cliffs and limestone mountains. As with so many flowers with a hairy calyx, it was used in the 16th century to dress wounds and to stop bleeding.

Sainfoin *(Onobrychis viciifolia)* is a British native legume and was widely cultivated as a forage crop. Its name is French, meaning 'wholesome or good hay', and it was coined into English in the 17th century.

Vetches are climbing or, often, scrambling plants with pinnate leaves, more-or-less long, flat pods and tendrils—sometimes branched—at the end of the leaves. It is the tendrils to look for when checking identification. The most commonly found is **Tufted Vetch** *(Vicia cracca)*. Pliny was not sure of its identity so he called it *cracca,* his standard term for plants of doubtful identity. Hairy Tare *(V. hirsuta)* has fewer and smaller flowers. It is the down on the pods which gives it its name.

Tufted Vetch

Sainfoin

Horseshoe Vetch

Spotted Medick

Kidney Vetch

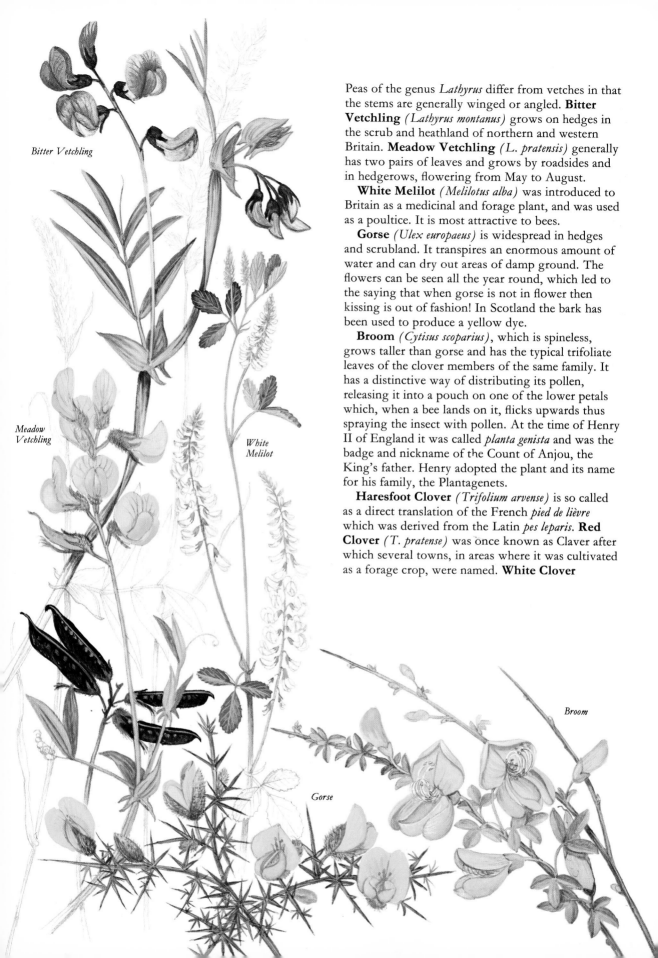

Bitter Vetchling

Meadow Vetchling

White Melilot

Gorse

Broom

Peas of the genus *Lathyrus* differ from vetches in that the stems are generally winged or angled. **Bitter Vetchling** *(Lathyrus montanus)* grows on hedges in the scrub and heathland of northern and western Britain. **Meadow Vetchling** *(L. pratensis)* generally has two pairs of leaves and grows by roadsides and in hedgerows, flowering from May to August.

White Melilot *(Melilotus alba)* was introduced to Britain as a medicinal and forage plant, and was used as a poultice. It is most attractive to bees.

Gorse *(Ulex europaeus)* is widespread in hedges and scrubland. It transpires an enormous amount of water and can dry out areas of damp ground. The flowers can be seen all the year round, which led to the saying that when gorse is not in flower then kissing is out of fashion! In Scotland the bark has been used to produce a yellow dye.

Broom *(Cytisus scoparius)*, which is spineless, grows taller than gorse and has the typical trifoliate leaves of the clover members of the same family. It has a distinctive way of distributing its pollen, releasing it into a pouch on one of the lower petals which, when a bee lands on it, flicks upwards thus spraying the insect with pollen. At the time of Henry II of England it was called *planta genista* and was the badge and nickname of the Count of Anjou, the King's father. Henry adopted the plant and its name for his family, the Plantagenets.

Haresfoot Clover *(Trifolium arvense)* is so called as a direct translation of the French *pied de lièvre* which was derived from the Latin *pes leparis*. **Red Clover** *(T. pratense)* was once known as Claver after which several towns, in areas where it was cultivated as a forage crop, were named. **White Clover**

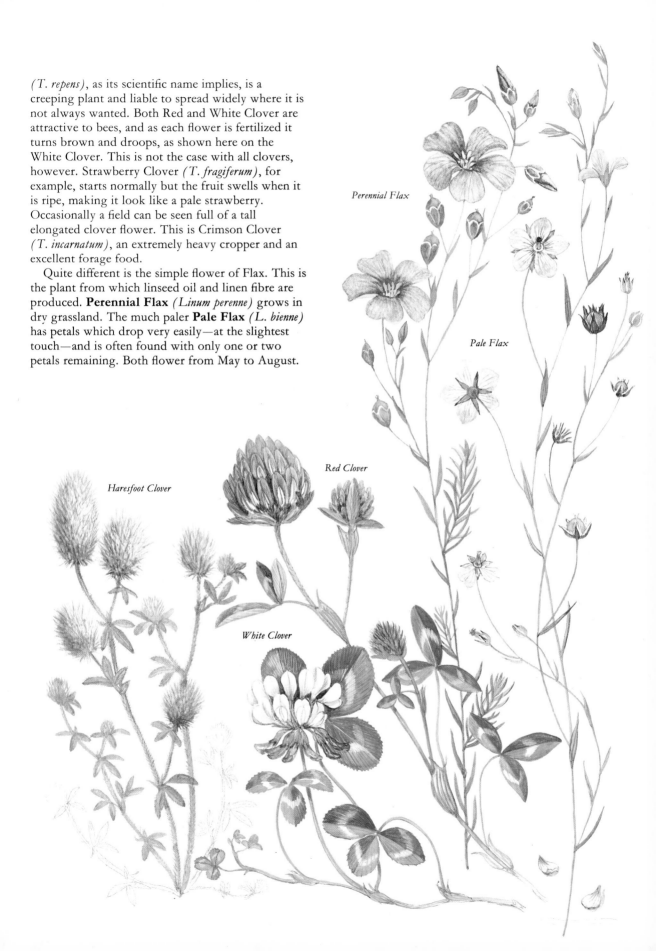

(*T. repens*), as its scientific name implies, is a creeping plant and liable to spread widely where it is not always wanted. Both Red and White Clover are attractive to bees, and as each flower is fertilized it turns brown and droops, as shown here on the White Clover. This is not the case with all clovers, however. Strawberry Clover (*T. fragiferum*), for example, starts normally but the fruit swells when it is ripe, making it look like a pale strawberry. Occasionally a field can be seen full of a tall elongated clover flower. This is Crimson Clover (*T. incarnatum*), an extremely heavy cropper and an excellent forage food.

Quite different is the simple flower of Flax. This is the plant from which linseed oil and linen fibre are produced. **Perennial Flax** (*Linum perenne*) grows in dry grassland. The much paler **Pale Flax** (*L. bienne*) has petals which drop very easily—at the slightest touch—and is often found with only one or two petals remaining. Both flower from May to August.

Perennial Flax

Pale Flax

Red Clover

Haresfoot Clover

White Clover

Dusky Cranesbill

Meadow Cranesbill

Bloody Cranesbill

The Geranium family

The Geranium family (Geraniaceae) is so called from the shape of the seed capsule, which resembles the beak of a crane—the word 'geranium' comes from the Greek for 'crane's bill', which, of course, is the name by which members of the family are known in Britain. It is a family which catapults its seeds, some plants being capable of throwing them up to twenty feet.

Many species were introduced to Britain from southern Europe, but **Meadow Cranesbill** *(Geranium pratense)* is probably native. Its range extends to Iceland and it is now spreading fast in North America. It grows in dry grassland on limey soil, flowers from June to September and dies down completely after seeding. It is a beautiful sight on some roadside verges and does well in the garden where it is easy to control and well worth growing. **Dusky Cranesbill** *(G. phaeum)* used to be considered a good wound herb, as were many plants of this family. It was probably a very early introduction and naturalized by the 16th century. It is often seen by the roadside in Central Europe. Both were grown by John Gerard, as was **Bloody Cranesbill** *(G. sanguineum)* which grows on sand dunes and limestone rocks and is often cultivated as a garden plant. The **Longstalked Cranesbill** *(G. columbinum)* has very long, thin flower stems and narrow, finely cut leaves.

More than a hundred other English names have been given to **Herb Robert** *(G. robertianum)* which grows in oak woods, hedges and verges. It has a strong foxy smell and the leaves turn red in winter. Named after Robert de Molesmes, an 11th-century healer and saint, it has a powerful astringent quality and was used to staunch wounds. It is a commoner weed than **Shining Cranesbill** *(G. lucidum)*, with its brilliant leaves and very small flowers, which grows on shady walls, banks and waste ground. One of the most delicately veined species is **Pencilled Cranesbill** *(G. versicolor)* which was introduced from Italy in the 17th century and is now naturalized in the hedges of Devon and Cornwall. Another species introduced from southern Europe, at the end of the 18th century, is **Hedgerow Cranesbill** *(G. pyrenaicum)*. A common roadside plant, it is also to be found in waste places, in company perhaps with **Dovesfoot Cranesbill** *(G. molle)*, a velvety plant and as such much used as a wound herb. It grows on arable land in corn-growing areas. **French Cranesbill** *(G. endressii)* escaped from gardens and is now naturalized in various parts of the country. **Cut-leaved Cranesbill** *(G. dissectum)* is another weed of arable land and dry grassland throughout Europe. It flowers from May to September.

1. *Longstalked Cranesbill*
2. *Herb Robert*
3. *Shining Cranesbill*
4. *Pencilled Cranesbill*
5. *Hedgerow Cranesbill*
6. *Dovesfoot Cranesbill*
7. *French Cranesbill*
8. *Cut-leaved Cranesbill*

1   2   3   4   5   6   7   8

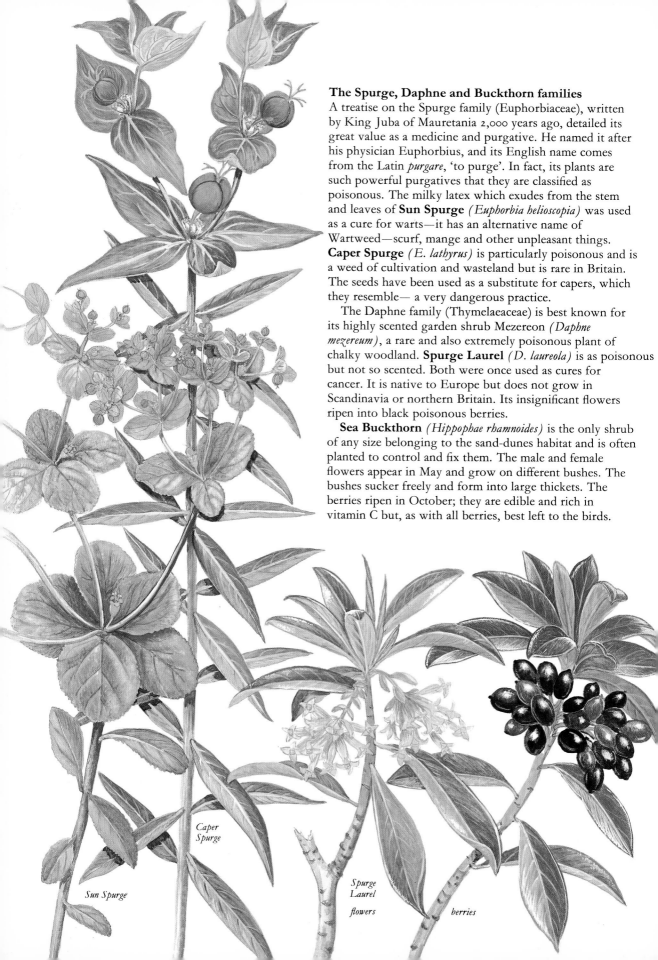

The Spurge, Daphne and Buckthorn families

A treatise on the Spurge family (Euphorbiaceae), written by King Juba of Mauretania 2,000 years ago, detailed its great value as a medicine and purgative. He named it after his physician Euphorbius, and its English name comes from the Latin *purgare*, 'to purge'. In fact, its plants are such powerful purgatives that they are classified as poisonous. The milky latex which exudes from the stem and leaves of **Sun Spurge** *(Euphorbia helioscopia)* was used as a cure for warts—it has an alternative name of Wartweed—scurf, mange and other unpleasant things.

Caper Spurge *(E. lathyrus)* is particularly poisonous and is a weed of cultivation and wasteland but is rare in Britain. The seeds have been used as a substitute for capers, which they resemble— a very dangerous practice.

The Daphne family (Thymelaeaceae) is best known for its highly scented garden shrub Mezereon *(Daphne mezereum)*, a rare and also extremely poisonous plant of chalky woodland. **Spurge Laurel** *(D. laureola)* is as poisonous but not so scented. Both were once used as cures for cancer. It is native to Europe but does not grow in Scandinavia or northern Britain. Its insignificant flowers ripen into black poisonous berries.

Sea Buckthorn *(Hippophae rhamnoides)* is the only shrub of any size belonging to the sand-dunes habitat and is often planted to control and fix them. The male and female flowers appear in May and grow on different bushes. The bushes sucker freely and form into large thickets. The berries ripen in October; they are edible and rich in vitamin C but, as with all berries, best left to the birds.

Caper Spurge

Sun Spurge

Spurge Laurel flowers

berries

Sea Buckthorn

Female flower

Male flower

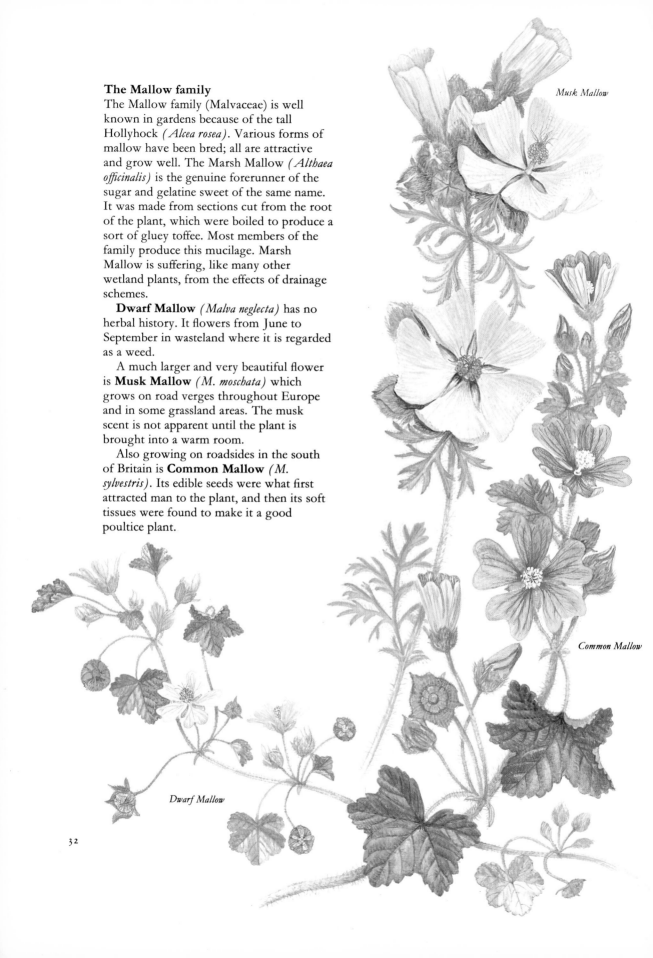

The Mallow family

The Mallow family (Malvaceae) is well
known in gardens because of the tall
Hollyhock *(Alcea rosea)*. Various forms of
mallow have been bred; all are attractive
and grow well. The Marsh Mallow *(Althaea
officinalis)* is the genuine forerunner of the
sugar and gelatine sweet of the same name.
It was made from sections cut from the root
of the plant, which were boiled to produce a
sort of gluey toffee. Most members of the
family produce this mucilage. Marsh
Mallow is suffering, like many other
wetland plants, from the effects of drainage
schemes.

Dwarf Mallow *(Malva neglecta)* has no
herbal history. It flowers from June to
September in wasteland where it is regarded
as a weed.

A much larger and very beautiful flower
is **Musk Mallow** *(M. moschata)* which
grows on road verges throughout Europe
and in some grassland areas. The musk
scent is not apparent until the plant is
brought into a warm room.

Also growing on roadsides in the south
of Britain is **Common Mallow** *(M.
sylvestris)*. Its edible seeds were what first
attracted man to the plant, and then its soft
tissues were found to make it a good
poultice plant.

Musk Mallow

Common Mallow

Dwarf Mallow

St John's Wort family

St John's Wort (Guttiferae) is a family with much legend attached to it. Many magical attributes are also to its credit. Herbs of St John were said to protect animals, buildings, man and his family against demons and evil spirits, and on St John's Eve, 23rd June, they were passed through smoke to make them even more powerful.

Slender St John's Wort *(Hypericum pulchrum)* is found on heathland scrub, and it is one of the smallest of the family. The leaves have tiny translucent dots on them.

Perforate St John's Wort *(H. perforatum)*, sometimes called Common St John's Wort, is considerably larger. It acquired its name because the oil glands within the leaf extend almost from surface to surface, making the leaf appear to have holes in it. Because of the scent given off by the oil, it is sometimes also called Rosin Rose. The leaves are used to scent clothes-cupboards and books and are said to discourage moths.

Marsh St John's Wort *(H. elodes)* grows mainly near ponds and backwaters and in damp grassland but, in common with so many other plants found in wetlands, is endangered because of drainage schemes.

Tutsan *(H. androsaemum)*, looking rather like a small version of the famous Rose of Sharon *(H. calycinum)*, with red spots on the stems, flowers from June to August and produces beautiful berries. The English name comes from the French *tout sain*, 'all healthy'. This description reflects its previous herbal value. It grows rather in isolation and does not form large thickets or colonies, and can be found in shaded woods, mainly in western areas.

Perforate St John's Wort

Slender St John's Wort

Marsh St John's Wort

Tutsan flower

Tutsan berries

33

The Violet family

Violets and pansies are members of the same family (Violaceae), the main difference between the two being the shape of the leaves. Violet leaves are generally heart-shaped whereas pansy leaves are deeply toothed, narrow and tapering, or lanceolate. The very fragrant Sweet Violet *(Viola odorata)* grows in woods, on scrubland and in some hedgerows. **Field Pansy** *(V. arvensis)* is a weed on cultivated ground, flowering from April to November.

One of the most beautiful of all this family is **Wild Pansy** *(V. tricolor)* which we have seen in a great many habitats but usually on bare ground at all altitudes up to 4,000 feet. It is often known as Heartsease, which is its 16th-century name and the one used by Shakespeare. Another name he used was Love-in-Idleness which Parkinson thought 'a foolish name'. It grew widely in cornfields, according to farmers of the day, and is the flower from which the modern garden pansy was developed.

The most common violet found in Britain is the **Common Dog Violet** *(V. riviniana)*. Many flowers not considered to be the best, in the days when so many names were being coined, were often given the label of being good only for animals, and so it is with this one. Gerard named it thus because he knew and preferred the scented Sweet Violet and considered this one fit only for dogs. It hybridizes with other violets, making identification difficult.

There is no problem in identifying **Dwarf Pansy** *(V. kitaibeliana)*. It is rare and in Britain must be left to grow in its few homes without disturbance from anything but the Atlantic gales with which it copes so well.

Field Pansy

Wild Pansy

Common Dog Violet

Heath Dog Violet

Dwarf Pansy

Marsh Violet

Marsh Violet *(V. palustris)* grows in heath and moor bogs and flowers from April to July. Like other marshland plants, it faces problems because of drainage schemes. No such problems exist for the lovely pale-blue **Heath Dog Violet** *(V. canina)* which grows on dry heaths and coastal sand dunes. It has a close habit of growth and its seeds attract ants which collect and store them.

The Gourd family
The only member of the Gourd family (Cucurbitaceae) to be found wild in Britain is **White Bryony** *(Bryonia cretica)*. It grows in hedges from a large parsnip-type root which in days gone by was sometimes called Mandrake. It is in no way related to Black Bryony *(Tamus communis)* which is a member of the Yam family and illustrated on page 62. White Bryony climbs, by means of tendrils, in hedgerows and on scrubland. The name is derived from the old Greek word *bruo* meaning 'to burst forth', as the plant indeed does in the spring. The leaves are dull, as are the berries which are also extremely poisonous. The male and female flowers grow on separate plants. In this illustration the female flowers are shown above the male ones.

Cucumbers and marrows are also members of the Gourd family. Two other species are found wild in northern Europe—*Bryonia alba* is found in Germany, France and Scandinavia, while Prickly Cucumber *(Echinocystis lobata)* has been introduced to Germany from North America.

Female flowers

Male flowers

White Bryony

The Willowherb family

Rosebay Willowherb *(Epilobium augustifolium)* is a very common sight nowadays but it was rarely found outside gardens until about 1860. It was originally grown by the Victorians as a decorative flower until it was realized what an invasive weed it is. The growth of travel by train and later by car has helped to spread it along railway embankments and roadsides, as its light feathery seeds, capable of considerable periods of dormancy, are wafted along by breezes.

Other members of this family also spread rapidly, for example, New Zealand Willowherb *(E. brunnescens)*, which is a low-growing plant, was first recorded in Britain near Edinburgh in 1904 and is now widespread in Ireland and northern

Rosebay Willowherb

Alpine Willowherb

Rosebay seeds

36

and western Britain. The equally
enthusiastic American Willowherb
(*E. adenocaulon*) was first recorded in
Leicester in 1891 and is now
common on railway embankments
and wasteland. Willowherbs
hybridize freely but with no great
success. The results are often sterile
and stunted, frequently dying before
they can flower.

Alpine Willowherb (*E.
anagallidifolium*) grows on mossy
cushions in mountain areas and
flowers from June to August.

Contrasting completely in shape
and colour is another member of the
same family, the **Large-flowered
Evening Primrose** (*Oenothera
erythrosepala*) which was introduced
from North America as a garden
plant and which now grows by the
roadside, on banks, in waste places
and on dunes. In some areas it has
colonized newly built road verges.
The seeds can remain dormant for at
least forty years. It is likely that new
roadworks will bring them to the
surface where they will germinate.

How **Enchanter's Nightshade**
(*Circaea lutetiana*) became so called is
rather a mystery. In folklore it has
no connection with witches or
enchanters, but its French name is
herbe à la magicienne, and indeed the
scientific name comes from that of
the Greek enchantress Circe who
turned the followers of Odysseus
into pigs by giving them a drink
made from this plant. A persistent
and spreading weed, it is extremely
difficult to eradicate. Having
flowered and seeded, the main stem
dies, whereupon underground roots
form new plants. The seeds
themselves are spread by means of
barbs on the seed capsules, which
become caught up in the fur of
animals and the clothes of man.

Large-flowered Evening
Primrose

Enchanter's
Nightshade

The Carrot family

The Carrot family (Umbelliferae) has nearly 3,000 species throughout the world, most of them easily recognizable by their umbrella-type flower heads. Small, five-petalled flowers on stalks form either flat-topped or rounded umbels, the whole head being made up of many of these. Most of the family have white flowers, sometimes tinged with pink, but there are also several yellow species and other less typical plants. The leaves, which are generally pinnate, and the hard, dry seeds are a valuable guide to identification. Hedgerows and scrubland are their habitats.

Throughout history umbellifers have been useful plants. The seeds of some were burnt to freshen the atmosphere, and some are still used as spices and flavourings. The Wild Carrot *(Daucus carota)* is an ancestor of our modern carrot. The largest wild flower in Britain today is the Giant Hogweed *(Heracleum mantegazzianum)* which was introduced from southwest Asia and escaped to the wild. It can grow to a height of fifteen feet with an umbel eighteen inches across. Corn Parsley *(Petroselinum segetum),* also a member of this family, is a protected species.

The above examples demonstrate the great versatility of this family. Not all are good though, for Ground Elder *(Aegopodium podagraria)*, although edible, is one of the worst weeds of the garden and hardest to eradicate. Fool's Parsley *(Aethusa cynapium)* is poisonous and should be avoided. Both it and Hemlock *(Conium maculatum)* must be remembered when using any wild umbellifer for cooking.

Sanicle

Sea Holly

Marsh Pennywort

Three less typical umbellifers grow wild in Britain.
Sea Holly *(Eryngium maritimum)* was common
throughout Europe on sand dunes and shingle
beaches, but over-picking and uprooting are
eradicating it from beaches frequented by visitors. It
is very attractive to bees and butterflies. It was once
the source of considerable trade in the Colchester
area where the candied roots were sold as an
aphrodisiac and stimulant.

As unlike the rest of the family as Sea Holly is
Marsh Pennywort *(Hydrocotyle vulgaris)*. The only
species in the family to have round leaves, it grows
in damp grassland and shallow water throughout
Europe. It was once thought to cause liver rot in
sheep, but it is the liver fluke parasite in a water snail
that is guilty, not the flower. **Sanicle** *(Sanicula
europaea)* was once a herb of great medicinal value.
Its name comes from the Latin *sano*, 'to heal', and
was said 'to make whole and sound all inner hurts
and outward wounds'. It is a small refined-looking
plant which grows in and near deciduous woodlands
throughout Europe.

The conventional umbellifer plant—if there is such
a thing—is **Cow Parsley** *(Anthriscus sylvestris)* which
lines so many roads, growing in hedges and on
verges. The earliest flowering plant of the family, it
is one of the most attractive with its delicate umbels
of white flowers which have given it the more
attractive common name of Queen Anne's Lace. It is
closely related to Garden Chervil *(A. cerefolium)*
which is a delicious wild herb.

Two of the yellow umbellifers are illustrated
overleaf: **Wild Parsnip** *(Pastinaca sativa)*, an
ancestor of the domestic parsnip, is recognizable by
its thick coarse growth and broad-toothed leaflets.
Near the coasts of Britain, France and Germany
grows one of the older vegetables, **Alexanders**
(Smyrnium olusatrum), which was introduced to
Britain from the Mediterranean in the 16th century as
a pot herb and was soon established and naturalized.
Concentrations of it can still be found on the sites of
old monasteries and castles, confirming the locations
of the kitchen gardens. It is most noticeable in
autumn by the presence of the black spicy seeds. It
was once called Parsley of Alexandria, hence its
modern name.

Cow Parsley

Wild Parsnip

Alexanders seeds

Alexanders

The Wintergreen and Heath families

Common Wintergreen *(Pyrola minor)* is a member of a small family (Pyrolaceae) of only thirty species throughout the world. It has a history as a healing herb and grows in woods and marshes, on moors and mountains. It flowers from June to August in southern parts of Britain where it is locally common, but is much more widespread on the Continent. It is said that the name comes from the Greek *pyrus*, 'pear', after the similarity of the leaves.

Heathers belong to the Heath family, Ericaceae— the name is derived from the Greek word *ereikh*, 'heath', which sums up the habitat, for the plants grow on heathland, moorland and open woodland on acid soils. **Bell Heather** *(Erica cinerea)* grows on dry heath and acid moor, flowering from July to September. It is fairly widespread on the west coast of Britain, especially in Scotland, and it thrives in Continental Europe on the west and north coasts of France and Belgium. **Cross-leaved Heath** *(E. tetralix)* is so called because the narrow linear leaves are formed in a cross on the stem. In contrast to Bell Heather, it grows on wet moors and dune slacks primarily in the north and west areas of Britain and on the northern coastal belt of the Continent.

Heather *(Calluna vulgaris)*, sometimes called Ling, is a small shrub common throughout Europe, and has been useful economically ever since Neolithic times for beds, thatch, fuel, baskets, rope and brooms. An English alternative name was Broom, and the word *Calluna* is derived from the ancient Greek *kallona* meaning 'to cleanse'—presumably with a heather broom. Heather was also used to make an orange dye and even to flavour beer. It grows on heaths, moors and dunes, in open birch and pine woodland and on upper moors in Britain. It is regularly burnt to provide a good crop of new shoots for grouse to eat.

There are several other forms of heather and all grow in their own specialized areas. Cornish Heath *(Erica vagans)* grows only in western areas of France besides its special place in Cornwall, and Dorset Heath *(E. ciliaris)* is found in similar areas. There are also some small shrubby plants like Bilberry, Cowberry and Cranberry, which grow in association with heathers. Larger shrubs which are also members of the Heath family and which have been bred for growing in gardens include rhododendrons and azaleas.

Common Wintergreen

Bell Heather

Cross-leaved Heath

Heather

41

The Primrose family

The Primrose family (Primulaceae) is altogether a beautiful one, best known for the species of the same name but including such delightful plants as Cyclamen, Scarlet Pimpernel and Alpine Snowbell.

Oxlip *(Primula elatior)* has been growing in Europe for many centuries but is rare in Britain, now found in only one place where it is locally common, the chalky boulder clay of East Anglia. It is often confused with the more common False Oxlip which is a hybrid of Primrose and Cowslip. It was noticed in the 16th century that the **Cowslip** *(P. veris)* grew particularly well in the close vicinity of cowpats, called then cow slips or flops, and so the name was coined.

The **Primrose** *(P. vulgaris)* has always been the acknowledged harbinger of spring. It has the most nostalgic scent of all the family and is something to look forward to during the dull winter months. It is not invariably pale yellow as there is a purple form which grows naturally in Wales and the north of England and a dusky pink we personally like to consider a wild Cornish form. There are many suggestions for the derivation of the name. One is that it comes from the Latin *prima rosa*, 'first rose'; another that the old French name *Primverole* was anglicized to Prymrose and then Primrose.

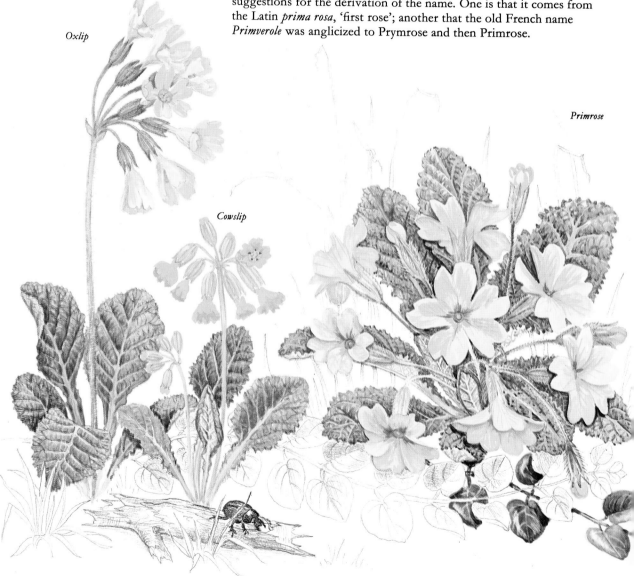

Oxlip

Primrose

Cowslip

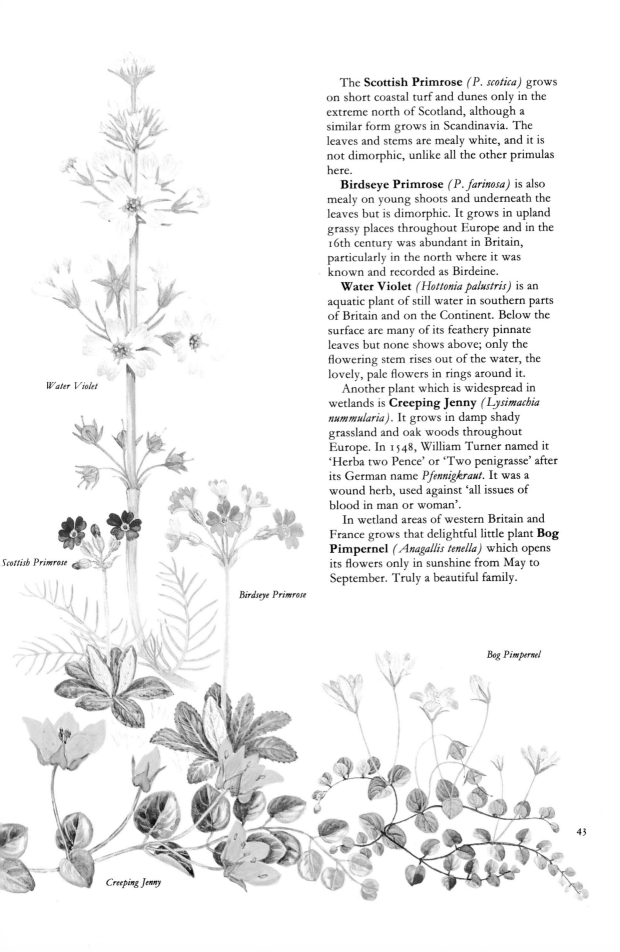

The **Scottish Primrose** *(P. scotica)* grows on short coastal turf and dunes only in the extreme north of Scotland, although a similar form grows in Scandinavia. The leaves and stems are mealy white, and it is not dimorphic, unlike all the other primulas here.

Birdseye Primrose *(P. farinosa)* is also mealy on young shoots and underneath the leaves but is dimorphic. It grows in upland grassy places throughout Europe and in the 16th century was abundant in Britain, particularly in the north where it was known and recorded as Birdeine.

Water Violet *(Hottonia palustris)* is an aquatic plant of still water in southern parts of Britain and on the Continent. Below the surface are many of its feathery pinnate leaves but none shows above; only the flowering stem rises out of the water, the lovely, pale flowers in rings around it.

Another plant which is widespread in wetlands is **Creeping Jenny** *(Lysimachia nummularia)*. It grows in damp shady grassland and oak woods throughout Europe. In 1548, William Turner named it 'Herba two Pence' or 'Two penigrasse' after its German name *Pfennigkraut*. It was a wound herb, used against 'all issues of blood in man or woman'.

In wetland areas of western Britain and France grows that delightful little plant **Bog Pimpernel** *(Anagallis tenella)* which opens its flowers only in sunshine from May to September. Truly a beautiful family.

Water Violet

Scottish Primrose

Birdseye Primrose

Bog Pimpernel

Creeping Jenny

43

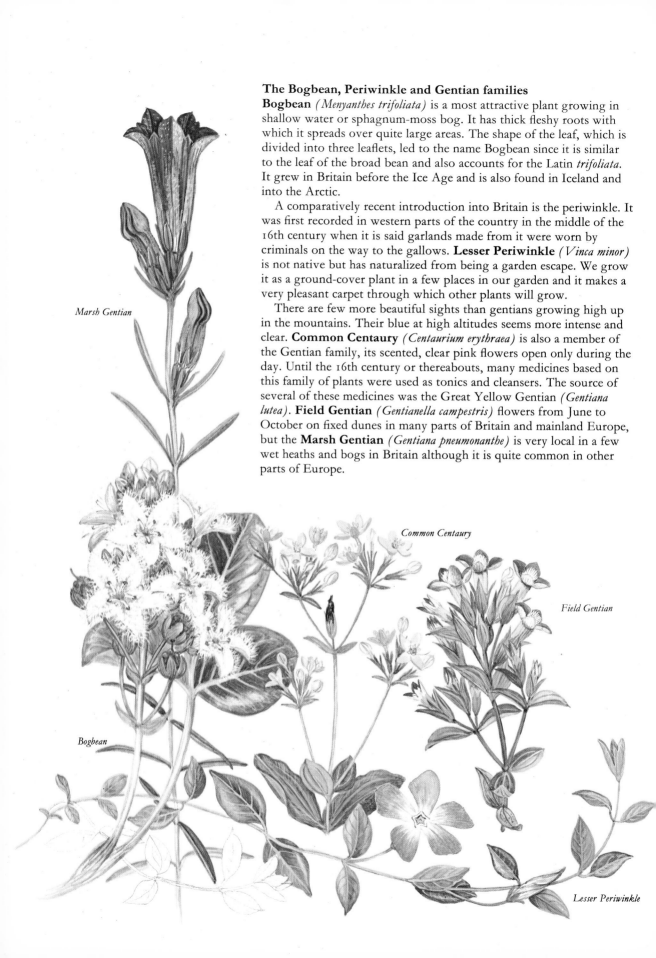

The Bogbean, Periwinkle and Gentian families

Bogbean *(Menyanthes trifoliata)* is a most attractive plant growing in shallow water or sphagnum-moss bog. It has thick fleshy roots with which it spreads over quite large areas. The shape of the leaf, which is divided into three leaflets, led to the name Bogbean since it is similar to the leaf of the broad bean and also accounts for the Latin *trifoliata*. It grew in Britain before the Ice Age and is also found in Iceland and into the Arctic.

A comparatively recent introduction into Britain is the periwinkle. It was first recorded in western parts of the country in the middle of the 16th century when it is said garlands made from it were worn by criminals on the way to the gallows. **Lesser Periwinkle** *(Vinca minor)* is not native but has naturalized from being a garden escape. We grow it as a ground-cover plant in a few places in our garden and it makes a very pleasant carpet through which other plants will grow.

There are few more beautiful sights than gentians growing high up in the mountains. Their blue at high altitudes seems more intense and clear. **Common Centaury** *(Centaurium erythraea)* is also a member of the Gentian family, its scented, clear pink flowers open only during the day. Until the 16th century or thereabouts, many medicines based on this family of plants were used as tonics and cleansers. The source of several of these medicines was the Great Yellow Gentian *(Gentiana lutea)*. **Field Gentian** *(Gentianella campestris)* flowers from June to October on fixed dunes in many parts of Britain and mainland Europe, but the **Marsh Gentian** *(Gentiana pneumonanthe)* is very local in a few wet heaths and bogs in Britain although it is quite common in other parts of Europe.

Marsh Gentian

Common Centaury

Field Gentian

Bogbean

Lesser Periwinkle

The Bindweed family

The familiar and, by gardeners, dreaded weed which winds and binds itself in and around other flowers and shrubs is well known. It is seen in hedgerows, on shingle or sandy beaches, in woodland and in arable land where it tangles itself and the sown crop into a solid mass. The member of the Bindweed family (Convolvulaceae) found on shingle beaches is the species **Sea Bindweed** *(Calystegia soldanella)* which also grows on sand dunes where its spreading roots help to bind and stabilize. The young shoots used to be gathered as a poor substitute for samphire. While in flower, from June to September, it will frequently be found with only its leaves because rabbits, which are particularly partial to the flowers, will not eat them.

The **Great Bindweed** *(C. sylvatical)*, illustrated overleaf, has large white flowers and inflated bracts. The beautiful flowers, which are sometimes pink or have pink stripes, are shown to best effect when the plant grows enthusiastically and anti-clockwise up the stay wire of a telephone pole. It has been shown that when growing with its usual vigour it will twine a full circle up such a wire in one and a half to two hours. It appears on waste ground and is most commonly found near human habitats. First recorded in 1548 by William Turner as a British wild flower, it was even then a pestilential garden weed.

Only one of the Bindweed family shown here is scented and that is **Field Bindweed** *(Convolvulus arvensis)*. It has alternative names which reflect countrymen's opinions of it: Withy Wind because it winds the withy, or willows, together, and Devil's Guts, coined from the German *Teufels Nohgern*. It spreads on bare arable ground and its capability is prodigious. In one season it has been known to cover thirty square yards.

Sea Bindweed

Great Bindweed

Field Bindweed

The Bedstraw family

The Bedstraw family (Rubiaceae) is the one whose plants stick to our clothes and whose seeds become impossibly enmeshed in the coats of our dogs. The stems of the coarse-growing **Wild Madder** *(Rubia peregrina)* have sharp downward-pointing prickles by which it climbs and scrambles over low-growing herbage near sea cliffs. The broad leaves are glossy and also have prickles. The seed is contained in a distinctive black berry.

Common Cleavers *(Galium aparine)* is a hedgerow plant. Because it was fed to geese, it is also called Goosegrass. In Gerard's time, the 16th century, he said, 'Women do usually make potage of Cleavers with a little oatmeal to cause lankeness'. Slimming is not new!

That **Lady's Bedstraw** *(G. verum)* was used to make junket, until the 17th century when it was replaced by rennet, is confirmed by its old French name of *caille-lait* and the Dutch *melklob*. In Chaucer's time beds were made of straw and Bedstraw, and according to a northern European legend Lady's Bedstraw was used with bracken as bedding in Christ's manger. The bracken refused to accept the Child so lost its scent, but the Bedstraw, then white, turned golden and its scent was increased.

The flower of **Woodruff** *(G. odoratum)* contains a chemical called coumarin which imparts the lovely scent of hay. In the Middle Ages it was used as a strewing herb.

Heath Bedstraw *(G. saxatile)* is found only on acid heath or moor and is the smallest and daintiest of this very pleasant, if troublesome, family.

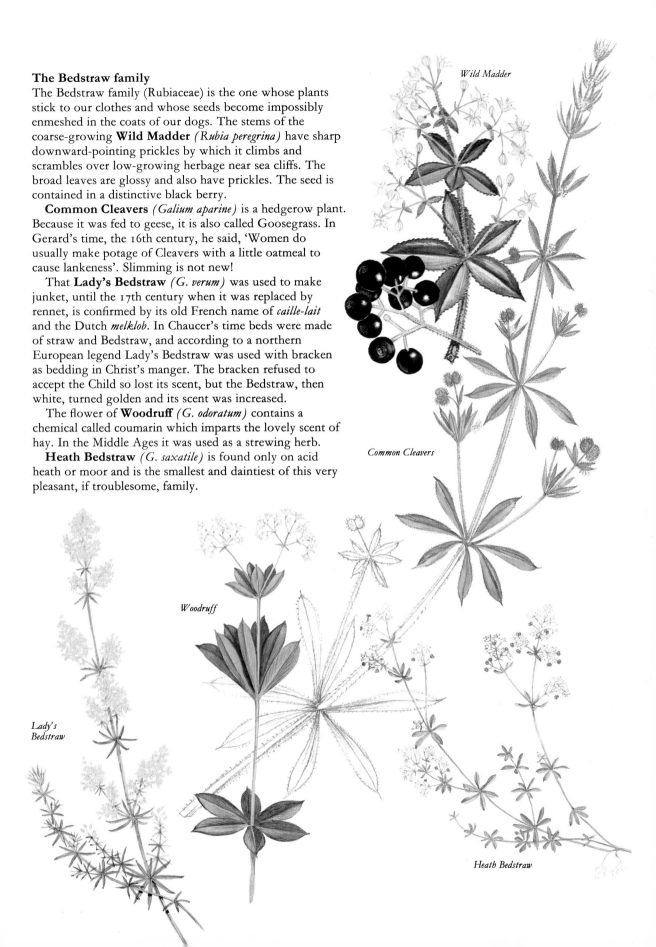

Wild Madder

Common Cleavers

Woodruff

Lady's Bedstraw

Heath Bedstraw

Borage

*Green
Alkanet*

*Changing
Forgetmenot*

*Early
Forgetmenot*

*Water
Forgetmenot*

The Borage family

Nearly all the plants in the Borage family
(Boraginaceae) are hairy on the leaves and stems and
often produce pink flowers which turn to blue as
they mature. There is no purer blue than **Borage**
(Borago officinalis) itself. Native to the Mediterranean
region, it was introduced to Britain very early as a
pot herb with medicinal qualities. It was said to be a
stimulant and 'to drive away melancholie' but its
chief virtue is as a flavouring for drinks. It is not as
common in the wild as it used to be as a garden
escape, but is unmistakable when found, generally
growing in dry bare places. A plant of it grown in a
herb garden will provide many flowers full of nectar
for bees which are very attracted to it.

Green Alkanet *(Pentaglottis sempervirens)* is a
flower of the hedgerow which has naturalized in
southwest Britain, having been introduced in the
Middle Ages as a dye plant. Despite its English
name, the root provides a brilliant red dye which
substantiates the derivation of the name as being
from the Spanish *alcanna* which in turn comes from
the Arabic *al henna*, the henna plant. This is the
source of the dye used by the women of Ancient
Egypt as a cosmetic and used again today for tinting
hair.

The most familiar flower of the family is the
forgetmenot, three species of which are illustrated
here. The name is said to come from a translation of
the 16th-century German name *Vergissmeinnicht*
which the French translated to *ne m'oubliez mye* and
which Samuel Taylor Coleridge coined in a poem in
1802 as 'Forget-me-not'. As the flower unwinds it
has a certain resemblance to a scorpion's tail, hence
the alternative name of Scorpion Grass.

Early Forgetmenot *(Myosotis ramosissima)* is the
smallest, and we have found it growing on the Isles
of Scilly, with the minute viola, the Dwarf Pansy,
both of them only one or two centimetres high and
exposed to the full fury of the Atlantic gales. As a
contrast, **Water Forgetmenot** *(M. scorpioides)* is one
of the largest-flowering species and grows in wet
places to a height of twelve inches. **Changing
Forgetmenot** *(M. discolor)* differs from the rest of
the genus by having yellow flowers which turn to
blue from May to June, when the other species also
will be flowering.

The Labiate family

The Labiate family (Labiatae) is one of the most important since it includes many species of herbs, such as mint, marjoram, sage, thyme and basil, to mention just the best known. Until the introduction of hops from Holland, **Ground Ivy** (*Glechoma hederacea*) was used as a flavouring for beer. It grows in woodland, on hedges and bare ground throughout Europe, flowering from March to June when the beauty of the labiate, or two-lipped, flowers can be appreciated.

Self-heal (*Prunella vulgaris*) is a flower of dry grassland and is more abundant on lime. It had a great reputation as a wound herb and cure for sore throats. Occasionally, but rarely, the flowers are pink or white.

The powder-blue flowers on a purplish spike belong to **Bugle** (*Ajuga reptans*) which is another wound herb from the Middle Ages. It appears in legends about thunder, lightning and fire; in Germany it is said that to bring it indoors when it flowers from April to June is to run the risk of fire consuming the house.

Wood Sage (*Teucrium scorodonia*) grows in woodland, heath and areas not on lime at heights up to 2,000 feet. It has little history as a culinary or medicinal herb, unlike other members of the family.

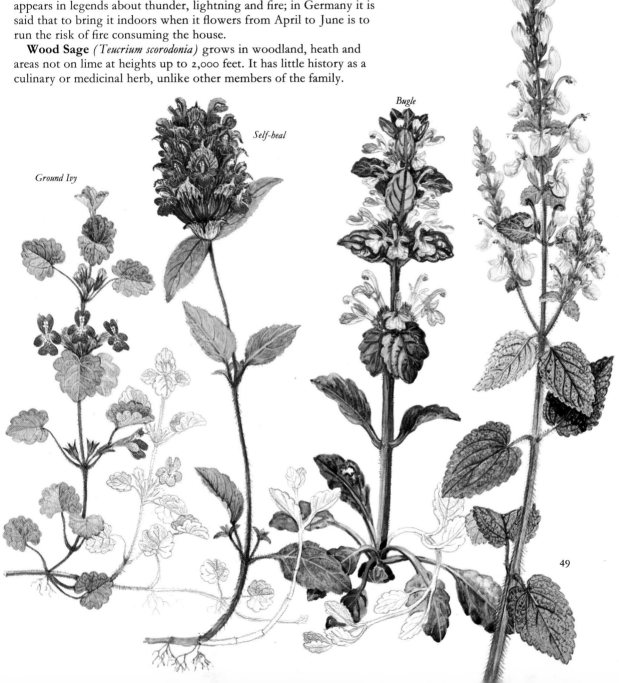

Wood Sage

Self-heal

Bugle

Ground Ivy

49

*Common
Hemp-nettle*

Betony

The flowers illustrated here show clearly the beauty of the Labiate family. Look into the individual flowers of any of these and you will see why we consider them to be just as lovely as some of the wild orchids which grow in Europe and why we are happy to have all the species described on this page growing together in our garden.

Several of the labiates are common in hedgerows where they are taken for granted. Those that are garden weeds are pulled up and cast on the compost heap without so much as a second look.

Hedge Woundwort *(Stachys sylvatica)* grows on hedges and is soon traced if it is in the garden because of the rather unpleasant smell which is given off when its square stem is crushed or broken. It blooms from June to October, when its flowers are best described as being beetroot in colour.

The **Common Hemp-nettle** *(Galeopsis tetrahit)*, which flowers from July to September, is paler and has swollen stems at the joint where the leaves and flower spikes branch out. Gerard called it Nettle Hemp in the late 16th century, but whether the fibre was ever used as a hemp we do not know.

Betony *(Betonica officioalis)* was first recorded in the 14th century and flowers from June to October. According to the 17-century herbalist Nicholas Culpeper, it was an exceedingly valuable herb, curing a wide range of ailments from headache to the bites of mad dogs.

Marsh Woundwort *(Stachys palustris)* is very orchid-like, with creamy marks on its lips. It is only faintly aromatic and hybridizes with Hedge Woundwort to produce flowers which are often of the colour of Hedge but with the narrow leaves of Marsh Woundwort.

50

*Hedge
Woundwort*

*Marsh
Woundwort*

*Hybrid of
Hedge and Marsh*

Galeopsis bifida

A very similar plant to Common Hemp-nettle, but without an English name, is **Galeopsis bifida** but it differs in that the hairs are more evenly spread and the flower is smaller, with the lower lip narrower and notched.

Yellow Archangel *(Lamiastrum galeobdolon)* is strong-smelling, creeping and invasive, with long runners which root at every node. It grows in woods and flowers from May to June.

Henbit Dead-nettle *(Lamium amplexicaule)* is a weed of light arable land, flowering from March to October, which has rounded leaves usually unstalked and half-clasping the stem. The **Red Dead-nettle** *(L. purpureum)* is a widespread garden weed which grows on waste ground as well. It is short and flowers from March to October. It is aromatic like the **White Dead-nettle** *(L. album)* which is the taller of the two and flowers on into November.

Like the White Dead-nettle, **Bastard Balm** *(Melittis melissophyllum)* often grows by roads. It is locally common in Britain only in the southwest where it was first recorded, in Devon, in 1650. It was originally called Bug Balm because of its unpleasant smell, but it is a beautiful-looking flower, the magenta-purple patches varying greatly from plant to plant.

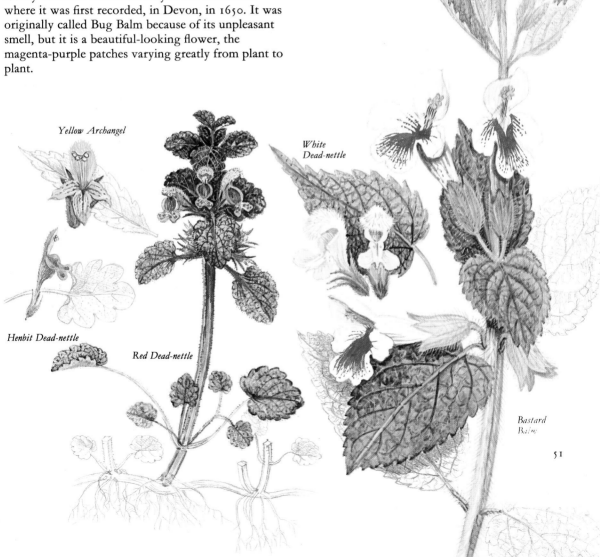

Yellow Archangel

White Dead-nettle

Henbit Dead-nettle

Red Dead-nettle

Bastard Balm

51

The Nightshade family

The Nightshade family (Solanaceae) includes the most important vegetables used by man—potato, tomato, pepper, aubergine—as well as some of the most poisonous plants, including Henbane and tobacco. The two species shown here are poisonous.

Bittersweet *(Solanum dulcamara)* can be found climbing or scrambling in hedgerows, on waste ground and on shingle beaches. It is extremely poisonous and a very ancient charm. German farmers would put garlands of the plant around the necks of their cattle to ward off witches and disease. It seems that these attributes had been handed down through the centuries because it has been found threaded on strings of date-palm leaf in Ancient Egyptian tombs—even in Tutankhamen's third coffin. In Germany it was also used by doctors against rheumatism and as a purgative, and in England Culpeper recommended it for dizziness.

The even more poisonous **Deadly Nightshade** *(Atropa bella-donna)* grows in scrub on limey soil and in woodland. Henry Lyte called it a 'naughtie and deadly plant', and Gerard suggested that 'being a plant so furious and deadly' it should be banished from the garden. In the 19th century it was realized that it contained a valuable ophthalmic drug, atropine, for dilating the pupils of the eyes. This property had already been discovered by the ladies of Venice in the Middle Ages, for they used it cosmetically to make their eyes appear larger and thus enhance their beauty—to make them *bella donnas*, hence the scientific name.

Bittersweet

Deadly Nightshade

The Figwort family

Digitalin, the drug used in the treatment of heart disease, comes from the Foxglove *(Digitalis purpurea)*, one of the members of the Figwort family (Scrophulariaceae).

The flowers of **Common Toadflax** *(Linaria vulgaris)* are similar to those of the antirrhinum, also a member of the family. It is most invasive and was a serious weed in flax fields when that was a major European crop. **Ivy-leaved Toadflax** *(Cymbalaria muralis)* introduced from southern Europe about 1617 as a garden plant, by the end of the 19th century was flourishing throughout the Thames basin and now flowers from April to November on walls throughout Europe.

Speedwells, well known and often grouped as birdseyes, form a genus of many species. **Germander Speedwell** *(Veronica chamaedrys)* flowers from April to June when its pronounced white 'eye' can be seen. The most recent of the genus to be recorded here, **Common Field Speedwell** *(V. persica)*, comes from western Asia and was first found in Berkshire in 1825. By the end of the century it had spread throughout Britain as a weed of cultivation. **Brooklime** *(V. beccabunga)*, whose name comes from the old English 'brok' (brook) and 'lemok' (plant), grows well in Scandinavia where it was called *bekkrbung*, 'brook-bung', as it was said to block up streams. Linnaeus presumably Latinized it to *beccabunga*.

Lousewort *(Pedicularis sylvatica)*, semi-parasitic on grass and sedge, flowers from April to July. It was once thought to infest cattle with lice, but in fact it contains a powerful natural insecticide.

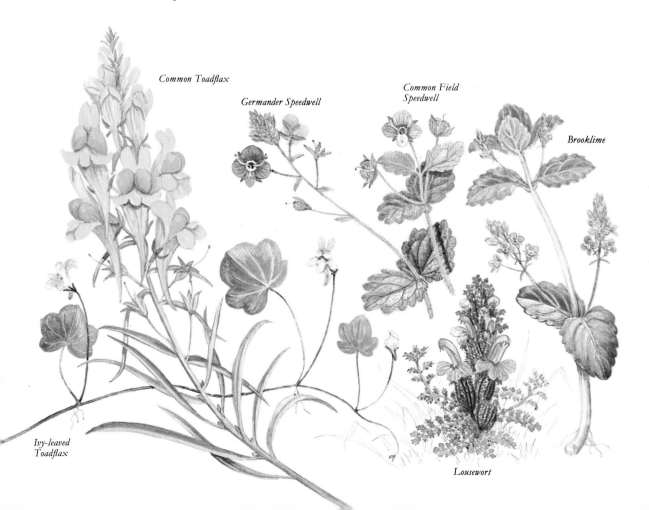

Common Toadflax

Germander Speedwell

Common Field Speedwell

Brooklime

Ivy-leaved Toadflax

Lousewort

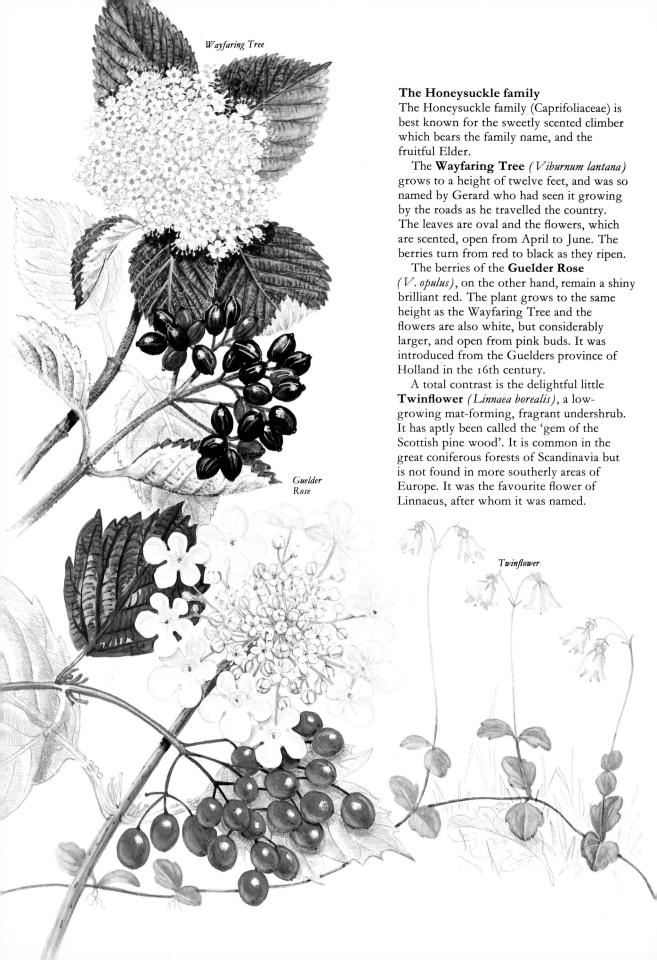

Wayfaring Tree

Guelder Rose

Twinflower

The Honeysuckle family

The Honeysuckle family (Caprifoliaceae) is best known for the sweetly scented climber which bears the family name, and the fruitful Elder.

The **Wayfaring Tree** *(Viburnum lantana)* grows to a height of twelve feet, and was so named by Gerard who had seen it growing by the roads as he travelled the country. The leaves are oval and the flowers, which are scented, open from April to June. The berries turn from red to black as they ripen.

The berries of the **Guelder Rose** *(V. opulus)*, on the other hand, remain a shiny brilliant red. The plant grows to the same height as the Wayfaring Tree and the flowers are also white, but considerably larger, and open from pink buds. It was introduced from the Guelders province of Holland in the 16th century.

A total contrast is the delightful little **Twinflower** *(Linnaea borealis)*, a low-growing mat-forming, fragrant undershrub. It has aptly been called the 'gem of the Scottish pine wood'. It is common in the great coniferous forests of Scandinavia but is not found in more southerly areas of Europe. It was the favourite flower of Linnaeus, after whom it was named.

The Teasel and Bellflower families

It was the Romans who first used the Teasel family (Dipsacaceae) as industrial tools for raising the nap on woollen cloth. The common **Teasel** *(Dipsacus fullonum)* has straight ends to the spines on the head, but the best for its industrial purpose and still in use, is Fuller's Teasel, a subspecies.

Like the Teasel, found in damp, grassy places, is **Devilsbit Scabious** *(Succisa pratensis)*. Culpeper reported it to be excellent for curing the plague, fever and freckles, among other things. It was said to annoy the Devil who took revenge by biting off the end of the taproot which is not as pointed as usual.

The **Field Scabious** *(Knautia arvensis)* flowers from June to October in dry, cornfield areas. It, too, had good qualities and was used to relieve sores, snake bites and other nasty complaints. The seeds are often spread by ants.

Sheepsbit Scabious *(Jasione montana)* superficially resembles the other scabious-named plants but is one of the Bellflower family (Campanulaceae). It grows in dry, grassy areas at altitudes up to 3,000 feet.

The bellflowers are beautiful, variable flowers. The **Harebell** *(Campanula rotundifolia)*, on page 3, is a weed difficult to eradicate from the garden. It grows on dry, chalky grassland as does the **Clustered Bellflower** *(C. glomerata)*, overleaf, whose alternative name is Dane's Blood because it was said to grow in areas attacked by Vikings. It is cultivated in gardens. The **Spreading Bellflower** *(C. patula)* can be found in woods and grassy places throughout Europe but is rare in Britain. **Nettle-leaved Bellflower** *(C. trachelium)* is in flower in midsummer like all the bellflowers and lasts well into September. It is a tall perennial, in contrast to the delightful little **Ivy-leaved Bellflower** *(Wahlenbergia hederacea)* which is found in damp woods and moors in most parts of Europe. **Heath Lobelia** *(Lobelia urens)* is very rare in Britain, protected in a nature reserve in Cornwall.

Teasel

Devilsbit Scabious

Field Scabious

Sheepsbit Scabious

Nettle-leaved Bellflower

Heath Lobelia

Spreading Bellflower

Clustered
Bellflower

Ivy-leaved
Bellflower

The Daisy family

The largest botanical family, covering the world with a fantastic array of flowers, is the Daisy family (Compositae). The **Daisy** *(Bellis perennis)* was known in Anglo-Saxon times as Day's Eye since it opens with the dawn and closes at dusk. Linnaeus named it *Bellis perennis,* 'beautiful perennial'.

Many of the family have good medicinal records and none better than **Feverfew** *(Tanacetum parthenium)*. In the 16th century it was found to be slightly analgesic and became the 'aspirin' of the day. It is a highly aromatic, short to medium perennial, growing on walls and in waste places and flowering from June to September.

Yarrow *(Achillea millefolium)* grows in grassland and has flowers, either white or pink, from June to November. Achilles found it cured his soldiers' wounds with its application, hence its generic name.

Sneezewort *(A. ptarmica)* grows in damp grassland on acid soil and flowers from July to September. It was used to combat toothache and, due to its ability to cause sneezing, as a snuff.

Scentless Mayweed *(Tripleurospermum inodorum)* is one of a group of plants which are all aromatic and growing on waste places but unlike them is not aromatic.

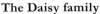

Sneezewort

Feverfew

*Scentless
Mayweed*

Daisy

Yarrow

57

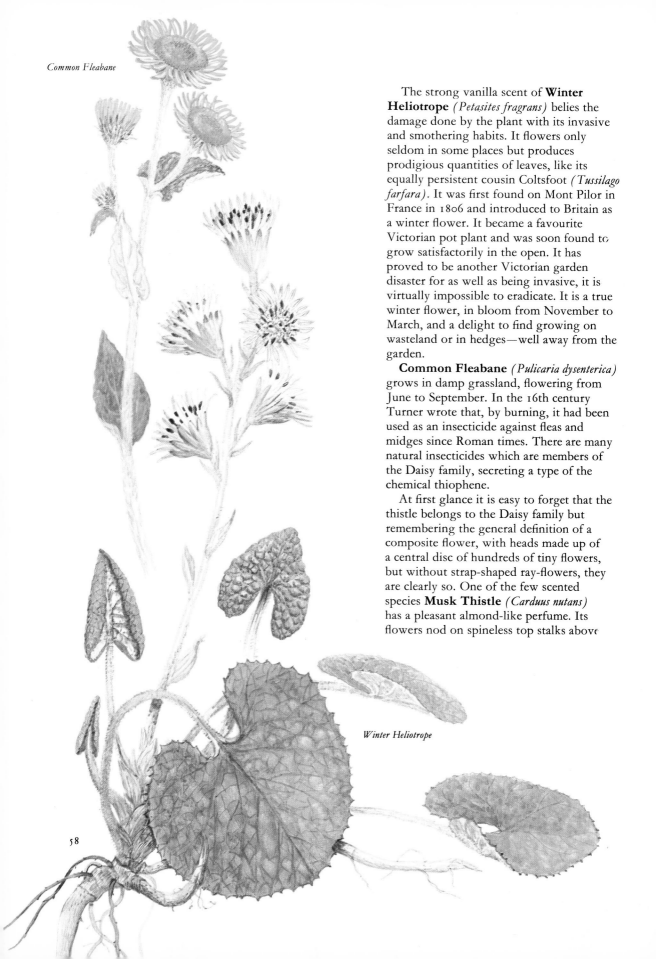

Common Fleabane

The strong vanilla scent of **Winter Heliotrope** *(Petasites fragrans)* belies the damage done by the plant with its invasive and smothering habits. It flowers only seldom in some places but produces prodigious quantities of leaves, like its equally persistent cousin Coltsfoot *(Tussilago farfara)*. It was first found on Mont Pilor in France in 1806 and introduced to Britain as a winter flower. It became a favourite Victorian pot plant and was soon found to grow satisfactorily in the open. It has proved to be another Victorian garden disaster for as well as being invasive, it is virtually impossible to eradicate. It is a true winter flower, in bloom from November to March, and a delight to find growing on wasteland or in hedges—well away from the garden.

Common Fleabane *(Pulicaria dysenterica)* grows in damp grassland, flowering from June to September. In the 16th century Turner wrote that, by burning, it had been used as an insecticide against fleas and midges since Roman times. There are many natural insecticides which are members of the Daisy family, secreting a type of the chemical thiophene.

At first glance it is easy to forget that the thistle belongs to the Daisy family but remembering the general definition of a composite flower, with heads made up of a central disc of hundreds of tiny flowers, but without strap-shaped ray-flowers, they are clearly so. One of the few scented species **Musk Thistle** *(Carduus nutans)* has a pleasant almond-like perfume. Its flowers nod on spineless top stalks above

Winter Heliotrope

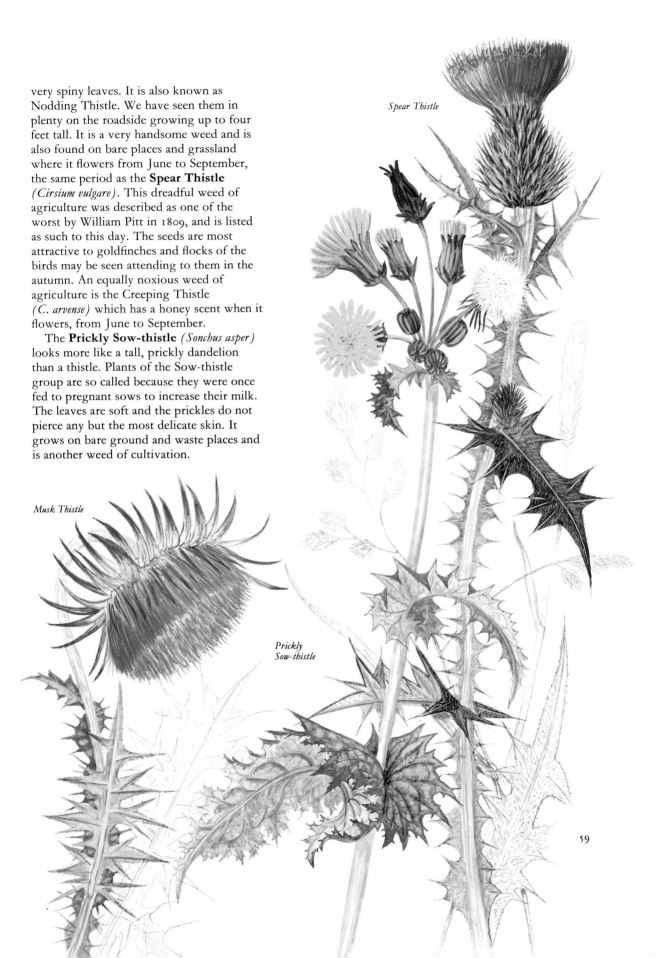

very spiny leaves. It is also known as
Nodding Thistle. We have seen them in
plenty on the roadside growing up to four
feet tall. It is a very handsome weed and is
also found on bare places and grassland
where it flowers from June to September,
the same period as the **Spear Thistle**
(Cirsium vulgare). This dreadful weed of
agriculture was described as one of the
worst by William Pitt in 1809, and is listed
as such to this day. The seeds are most
attractive to goldfinches and flocks of the
birds may be seen attending to them in the
autumn. An equally noxious weed of
agriculture is the Creeping Thistle
(C. arvense) which has a honey scent when it
flowers, from June to September.

The **Prickly Sow-thistle** *(Sonchus asper)*
looks more like a tall, prickly dandelion
than a thistle. Plants of the Sow-thistle
group are so called because they were once
fed to pregnant sows to increase their milk.
The leaves are soft and the prickles do not
pierce any but the most delicate skin. It
grows on bare ground and waste places and
is another weed of cultivation.

Spear Thistle

Musk Thistle

*Prickly
Sow-thistle*

59

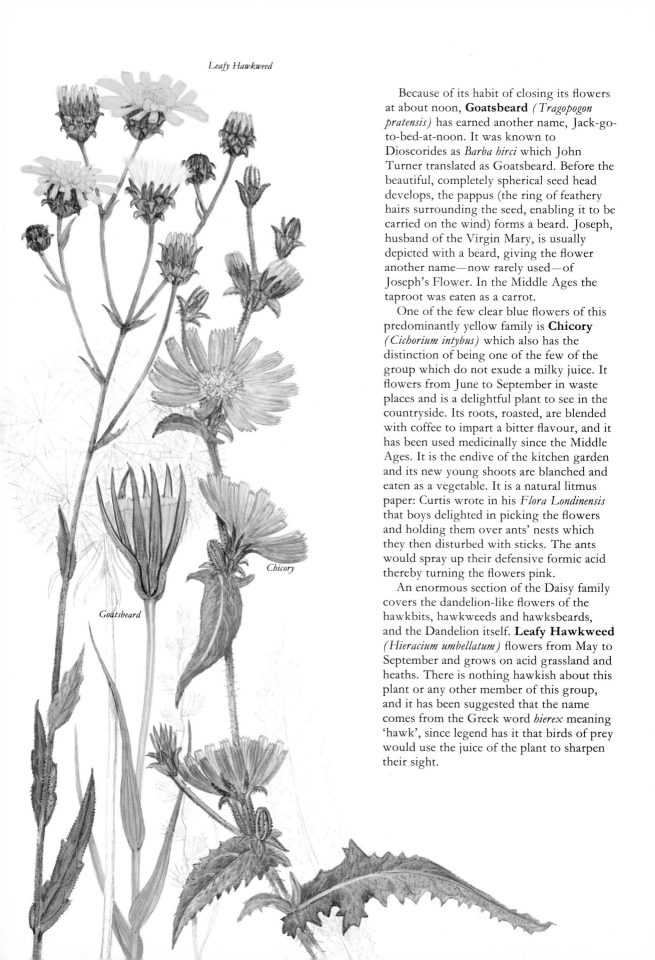

Because of its habit of closing its flowers at about noon, **Goatsbeard** *(Tragopogon pratensis)* has earned another name, Jack-go-to-bed-at-noon. It was known to Dioscorides as *Barba hirci* which John Turner translated as Goatsbeard. Before the beautiful, completely spherical seed head develops, the pappus (the ring of feathery hairs surrounding the seed, enabling it to be carried on the wind) forms a beard. Joseph, husband of the Virgin Mary, is usually depicted with a beard, giving the flower another name—now rarely used—of Joseph's Flower. In the Middle Ages the taproot was eaten as a carrot.

One of the few clear blue flowers of this predominantly yellow family is **Chicory** *(Cichorium intybus)* which also has the distinction of being one of the few of the group which do not exude a milky juice. It flowers from June to September in waste places and is a delightful plant to see in the countryside. Its roots, roasted, are blended with coffee to impart a bitter flavour, and it has been used medicinally since the Middle Ages. It is the endive of the kitchen garden and its new young shoots are blanched and eaten as a vegetable. It is a natural litmus paper: Curtis wrote in his *Flora Londinensis* that boys delighted in picking the flowers and holding them over ants' nests which they then disturbed with sticks. The ants would spray up their defensive formic acid thereby turning the flowers pink.

An enormous section of the Daisy family covers the dandelion-like flowers of the hawkbits, hawkweeds and hawksbeards, and the Dandelion itself. **Leafy Hawkweed** *(Hieracium umbellatum)* flowers from May to September and grows on acid grassland and heaths. There is nothing hawkish about this plant or any other member of this group, and it has been suggested that the name comes from the Greek word *hierex* meaning 'hawk', since legend has it that birds of prey would use the juice of the plant to sharpen their sight.

Chicory

Goatsbeard

The Lily family

Unless the leaves are crushed, the familiar onion scent is not always much in evidence with plants of the onion genus, part of the Lily family (Liliaceae). Chives *(Allium schoenoprasum)* is a member of the family, well known to gardeners.

Three-cornered Leek *(A. triquetrum)* was not recorded in Britain until late in the 18th century when it was found in west Cornwall and the Isles of Scilly. It was introduced from the Mediterranean and is such a pest to horticulture in some areas that growers can be fined for having it on their land. Woods and banks are its habitats where it flowers sometimes with **Ramsons** *(A. ursinum)* from April to June. On the Continent, particularly in the north and east, the name was *rams* which implies the same derivation as the Old English name of 'hramsan'. Gerard said the leaves made a good sauce to eat with fish but it was fit only for those with a strong constitution and for 'labouring men'. Two types of roots are produced: fibrous ones in the autumn absorbing nutrients and moisture; and in the spring fleshy taproots grow deep and eventually contract, thereby pulling the bulb farther into the ground. This ability to adjust its depth is shared by several bulbous plants, which is sometimes a help to those who may plant bulbs too shallow in their garden.

The **Sand Leek** *(A. scorodoprasum)* grows on sandy hedge banks and cultivated places throughout Europe. The long-stalked umbel also contains bulbils and may be seen from June to August when the flowers are blooming.

Crow Garlic *(A. vineale)* sometimes does not flower and then the bulbils take over the loosely formed umbel completely. It has been a noxious weed on the farm since Roman times and this has earned it its derogatory Crow epithet. It reproduces in five ways—from spring-sown seeds, aerial bulbils, underground bulbs growing in the axils, or 'armholes', of the leaves, offsets from the main bulb and from the main bulb itself.

A similar plant, with pink-purple flowers, **Keeled Garlic** *(A. carinatum)* was introduced into Britain in the 16th century.

In addition to having these troublesome pests, the Lily family has some of the most beautiful flowers there are, their names as lovely as the flowers.

Sand Leek

Keeled Garlic

Crow Garlic

Ramsons

Three-cornered Leek

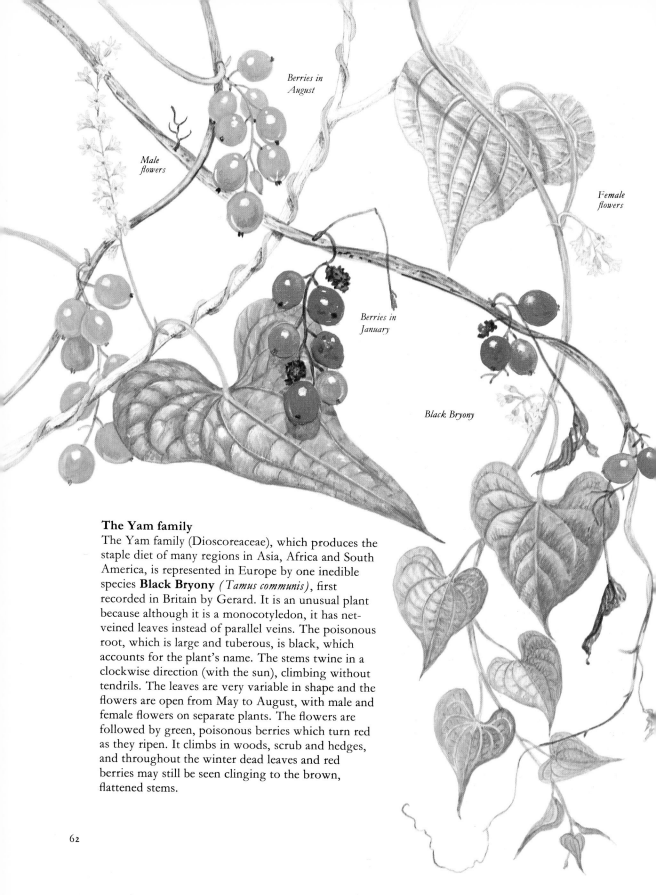

Berries in August

Male flowers

Female flowers

Berries in January

Black Bryony

The Yam family

The Yam family (Dioscoreaceae), which produces the staple diet of many regions in Asia, Africa and South America, is represented in Europe by one inedible species **Black Bryony** *(Tamus communis)*, first recorded in Britain by Gerard. It is an unusual plant because although it is a monocotyledon, it has net-veined leaves instead of parallel veins. The poisonous root, which is large and tuberous, is black, which accounts for the plant's name. The stems twine in a clockwise direction (with the sun), climbing without tendrils. The leaves are very variable in shape and the flowers are open from May to August, with male and female flowers on separate plants. The flowers are followed by green, poisonous berries which turn red as they ripen. It climbs in woods, scrub and hedges, and throughout the winter dead leaves and red berries may still be seen clinging to the brown, flattened stems.

The Iris, Daffodil and Lily families

The unfortunately named **Stinking Iris** *(Iris foetidissima)*, which grows in woodland, scrub and on sea cliffs in Britain and France, and the Yellow Iris *(I. pseudacorus)* are the two most common members of the Iris family (Iridaceae) growing wild in Britain. The Stinking Iris is so called because the leaves, when crushed, give off a sweet sickly smell which some think is like meat and accounts for an alternative name of the Roast Beef Plant. William Turner called it Spurgewort after its purgative powers. The berries in their open capsules last a long time.

'There hath beene great confusion among many of our moderne Writers of plants, in not distinguishing the manifold varieties of Daffodils', so wrote Parkinson in his *Paradisus* in 1629. He followed this statement with forty pages of classification which includes the **Wild Daffodil** *(Narcissus pseudonarcissus)*. Destruction of its habitat and removal to gardens has reduced this lovely spring flower to its modern comparative scarcity. With the exception of the very rare Tenby Daffodil *(N. obvallaris)* it is the only native wild daffodil in Britain. The other species are often garden escapes or naturalized and hybridized forms of plants originally introduced from southern Europe. The Snowdrop *(Galanthus nivalis)* and the Spring and Summer Snowflakes *(Leucojum vernum* and *L. aestivum)* are also members of the Daffodil family (Amaryllidaceae).

A beautiful plant of the Lily family is the **Lily of the Valley** *(Convallaria majalis)*. It has an unforgettable perfume and grows in fairly dry woodland in soil rich in humus. The bell-like flowers always nod to one side of the main flower stalk. Legend has it that they represent the tears of the Virgin Mary shed at the foot of the Cross.

The flowers of **Meadow Saffron** *(Colchicum autumnale)* appear in woods and damp grassy places in August and September before the leaves which grow in spring. The apparent stems of the flower are actually part of the flower itself, and are weak, resulting in a rather floppy habit of growth. They are often grown in gardens and are variously known as Naked Ladies, Naked Boys or Naked Nanny. Dioscorides said it was sufficiently poisonous to kill a man in one day. Apothecaries and herbalists proceeded with due caution and found it relieved gout. Beneficial under proper control, it is still listed as a palliative in the British Pharmacopoeia.

Stinking Iris and berries

Wild Daffodil

Meadow Saffron and bud

Lily of the Valley

63

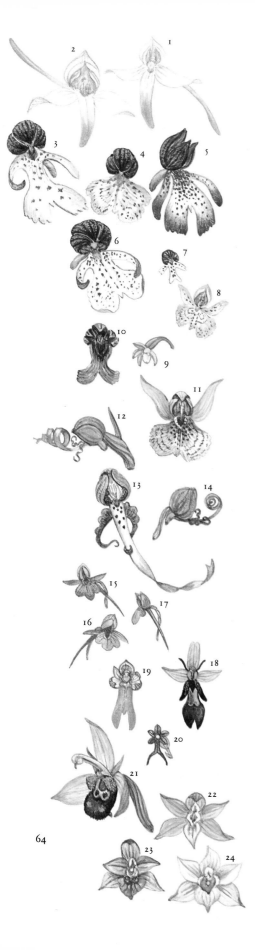

INTRODUCTION TO ORCHIDS

If there are any other flowers growing on this earth more certain to attract attention, more complicated in their construction, more fascinating, variable, vulnerable and altogether more captivating than orchids, then we have yet to find them. Their very name conjures up thoughts of wealth and luxury to many people, but we are not dealing with the exotic beauties of the rain forests or the cool sculptured perfections from the hot house, but the more simple wild orchids of Britain and Europe which are small and insignificant in comparison, and yet have such a strong appeal for us that annual orchid forays have become an essential part of our lives.

There are fifty species of orchid in this country and no other family can produce so many widely different and captivating flowers, each one an individual with its own peculiarities, smell, design, colour, shape, habit of growth and its own particular appeal. No flower family in Britain is more hunted and collected than the orchid; no other family has so many members on the list of protected species and so many more which may one day have to join them if they are to survive; and yet it is a family which also includes several species which are relatively common over a wide area of Britain and Europe, or in small localized communities.

The life story of the orchid is closely linked with that of a soil fungus called Mycorrhiza, meaning literally 'fungus root'. Mycorrhizal fungi obtain their nutrients parasitically from rotting and decaying vegetable matter in the soil, which we call humus. Part of the fungus lives outside the orchid, obtaining life-sustaining nutrients from the humus, which it passes on to the other part which penetrates deep into the roots and underground stems of the orchid

1 Lesser Butterfly Orchid
2 Greater Butterfly Orchid
3, 4, 5, 6 Lady Orchid showing variations of lip
7 Burnt Orchid
8 Heath Spotted Orchid
9 Coral-root Orchid
10 Birdsnest Orchid
11 Southern Marsh Orchid
12, 13, 14 Lizard Orchid
15, 16, 17 Fragrant Orchid
18 Fly Orchid
19 Common Twayblade
20 Lesser Twayblade
21 Bee Orchid
22 Narrow-lipped Helleborine
23 Broad-leaved Helleborine
24 Violet Helleborine

64

plant. The orchid has actually learnt to turn this parasitic situation to its own advantage, by digesting some of the advancing fungus and so acquiring an additional, valuable supply of second-hand food. The seed of the wild orchid is so fine and dust-like that it cannot store within itself any reserves of food, and so it too relies on this fungus to provide the nourishment for the tiny and slow-growing seedling, from the critical moment of germination until it has green leaves of its own to supply the food, which may not be for months, or even years in the case of some orchids. Many orchid seeds cannot even germinate, let alone grow, without the bolstering-up effect of the fungus.

The seedling starts life as a minute projection or bud, followed by the roots and then, after several months or years have passed, aerial stems and the first leaves are produced, but no flowers at this stage. The time between germination and flowering may be many years. Because of this, an orchid needs all the extra help the fungus can give it.

Most orchids die down after flowering, although some, like Autumn Lady's Tresses, develop their leaves during the autumn, and these remain all winter until the flower stem rises in the following year. The food required to nourish some orchid plants is stored in underground tubers, as in the case of the Marsh and Lizard Orchids. These have one tuber to produce food for leaves and flowers, and any nutrients over and above their requirements are stored in a second tuber which is produced later in the year to take over the role of the first one when it has exhausted its supply. Other orchids have an extensive network of underground stems and roots growing either horizontally or vertically, and in these they store their food. They include Lady's Slipper, the twayblades, Creeping Lady's Tresses and the helleborines. Another group, which includes the Bee, Fragrant and Early Purple Orchids, builds up a store of food during development but this becomes so depleted by the time the first flowers have been produced that some of the plants die of malnutrition. These species, called monocarpic, rely on the production of vast amounts of seed after one glorious flowering to carry on their race.

Root systems

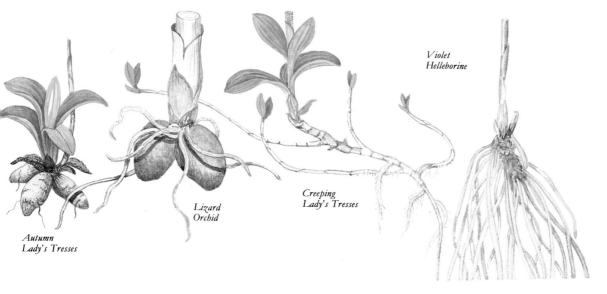

Violet Helleborine

Creeping Lady's Tresses

Lizard Orchid

Autumn Lady's Tresses

Some orchids are more heavily dependent than others on the fungus. If the woodland canopy above the Red Helleborine, for example, becomes too dense over the years, it has not enough light from which to manufacture chlorophyll and has to rely more and more on the fungus in order to survive, let alone to flower. Roots continue to grow but no stems appear, and this underground existence may continue for many years, some say for as long as twenty, until the felling of trees allows sufficient light to fall again upon the woodland floor, when the flowers will reappear as if by magic. Other orchids become self-supporting after they have passed the juvenile stage, notably the Common Twayblade and the Lady's Slipper.

At the opposite end of the scale there are three orchids in Britain which are dependent upon the fungus for the whole of their lives. These are called saprophytic orchids; all are leafless and so cannot manufacture food for themselves, a case of parasites living off parasites. They grow in deep, dense woodlands, in a soil very rich in humus from which the invader draws the food that feeds both itself and the host plant. This food is stored in the roots of the orchid and in the nodules which develop upon them until there is sufficient to produce a flower stem, although this may not occur every year. The three orchids are the Birdsnest—which is fairly regular in its flowering habits—the Common Coral-root, and the tiny, aptly named Ghost Orchid, of great rarity, with its pale almost transparent stem, its strange and not very beautiful flowers. The Ghost may bloom one year and then not be seen for a further ten or even twenty years.

Identification of orchids can be a problem because of their habit of hybridizing—particularly among the genus *Dactylorhiza*, the marsh and spotted orchids—and also because of many variations in colour and markings. A few orchids occasionally produce complete or partial albinos, mainly among the red, purple and pink-flowered species. Leaves can vary in the number of spots present but as a rule not in the actual shape, and some species can even produce plants with plain leaves.

Orchid flowers are intricate pieces of engineering, with the male and female organs joined together in a single column—one of the general characteristics of this family. The pollen produced by the orchids is as fine as dust, but instead of being in separate grains and blowing about in the wind it is fused into small groups called pollinia. Each mass—the size of a pin's

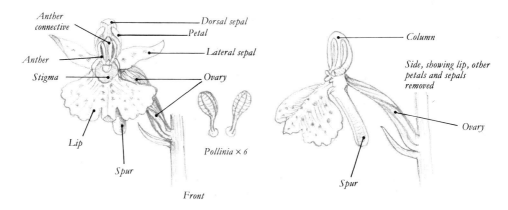

Anther connective

Anther

Stigma

Lip

Spur

Dorsal sepal

Petal

Lateral sepal

Ovary

Pollinia × 6

Front

Column

Side, showing lip, other petals and sepals removed

Ovary

Spur

head—contains thousands, even millions, of sticky pollen grains. The flowers are pollinated by many different species of insects, from tiny and not very intelligent, creeping ones, which visit the least complicated flowers, to the large butterflies and moths whose long proboscises are tailor-made to fit into the nectar-bearing spurs of some orchids. Finally, at the top end of the intelligence scale there are the highly developed bees which pollinate the most complicated and intricately designed flowers in the most efficient way possible. The pollination mechanism of the Common Twayblade serves as a good example. It has a nectar-producing groove down the centre of its small yellow-green lip, which provides delectable food for a variety of small, short-tongued insects, and it is one of those rare types of plants which is visited by ichneumon wasps. These visitors suck their way up the lip until they reach the point where it turns sharply downwards under the column. Here, a small beak-like projection, called the rostellum, is situated in such a position that the insect cannot fail to touch it, however lightly and briefly, and this triggers off an explosion which forces a drop of very sticky liquid from the tip of the rostellum on to the head of the insect, thus enabling the pollen, which is situated conveniently nearby, to become firmly attached to the insect on impact. The glue hardens in a matter of seconds, and the insect, being so startled by the whole procedure, usually flies away to a different plant, either to be bombarded yet again with more pollen or to cross-pollinate any mature and receptive flower whose sticky stigma is so positioned as to accept readily the clumps of pollen which are transferred to it from the insect's head. It needs only one pollinium or, at the most, two, placed on a receptive stigma to pollinate the vast numbers of ovules awaiting fertilization within a single ovary. It is astonishing that the entire world is not covered with orchids for each stem supports several flowers, from one or two in Spider Orchids to Lizard Orchids with up to seventy.

Orchids work hard to survive—some harder than others. A Common Twayblade produces a mere 500 seeds per capsule, but it can have as many as a hundred flowers on its stem. A Bee Orchid can average a staggering 10,000 and a really large capsule can produce 25,000 but there may not be more than six flowers on one stem. Tropical orchids outdo our European ones in a really spectacular way, for according to some experts the *Cymbidium* orchids may have as many as $1\frac{3}{4}$ million seeds in each capsule, and the Swan Orchid of America probably holds the record with 4 million in a capsule measuring six inches long and two inches in diameter. Self-pollination can take place in some orchids—it is common among the helleborines and also among the various *Ophrys*—but only as a last resort. For instance, as the flowers of the Bee Orchid mature, the pollen stalk shrivels and causes the pollen-bearing part to become dislodged from its bag, or container, and to bend over the stigma, after which any small breeze will cause the grains to touch and stick to the stigma.

When the seeds of orchids are ripe, the capsule containing them splits lengthways into six divisions, or valves, which are still attached at each end of the capsule. Any breeze or movement of the stem causes the seeds to be shaken out between the slits, and currents of warm air bear them to a great height and disperse them far and wide in the upper atmosphere from where they gently float down to land, we hope, on good earth.

The orchid which probably gives most pleasure when seen for the first time is the **Bee Orchid** *(Ophrys apifera)*. More common and widespread than the other members of its genus, the *Ophrys*, it is however elusive, sometimes flowering in large numbers in one particular area before disappearing for a few years or even forever. It is found mainly on chalk or limestone and sometimes on dunes and in woods. A rosette of leaves forms in the autumn and lasts throughout the winter. The flower stem, appearing in the spring, reaches heights from six inches to well over a foot, with as few as two flowers or as many as six and sometimes seven. They bloom from late May to June with their strangely beautiful, delicate-pink sepals and the velvet 'bee' body much in evidence. Many variations occur in the colour of the sepals and the marking on the lip. The flowers are said to be pollinated by bees which have also been observed trying to mate with the flower bee, but this we have not seen and we have heard doubts cast upon the role of the bee as the pollinator. It is far more commonly self-pollinated.

The **Wasp Orchid** *(O. apifera* var. *trollii)* is regarded as a subspecies of the Bee. It can be recognized by the pointed, dagger-shaped lip, the tip of which does not curl back as in the Bee Orchid. The colour of the lip is a mixture of hazy, mottled browns and green with a less noticeably velvety texture.

The **Late Spider Orchid** *(O. fuciflora)* is like the Bee in colour but the lip is larger, more spread out and curves slightly forward at the tip. It is frequently found in central and southern Europe and in very small colonies in the southeast tip of England where it grows only on chalkland with a short-cropped turf. Undergrazing has caused a marked decline in its numbers, making it exceedingly local and rare. It blooms from late May through June, growing from four to twelve inches tall. The two to six, beautiful flowers on the stem are so large that they make the little plant look top-heavy.

The **Early Spider Orchid** *(O. sphegodes)* is more easily overlooked, for it is sombre green and brown in colour and only three to nine inches tall as a rule, with two or three flowers on a stem, although up to six or seven have been found. The individual flowers, which appear in late April, are longlasting but do not always open at the same time. Its distribution is much the same as that of the Late Spider, although it was once probably widespread over several counties and can still be found in Dorset, Sussex and Kent. It grows well in coastal areas.

A favourite of ours is the **Fly Orchid** *(O. insectifera)* which is also easily overlooked. Its narrow, delicate, flowering stem is hung with small, brown 'flies' and grows from six to twenty-four inches tall. It is more widely distributed than the spiders although it is local and never common in Britain. It may be found near woodland edges, often in shade and always on chalk or limestone.

The **Frog Orchid** *(Coeloglossum viride)* is another inconspicuous plant. It is not really frog-like except in its colouring which varies from green to brownish, often tinged with red. Sometimes the whole plant, which is only a few inches tall, is suffused with this reddish colour. Widely distributed through central Europe and in Britain, although it grows in quite large numbers in a few small areas, it is not common. It is in flower from June to August and is pollinated by small insects including beetles.

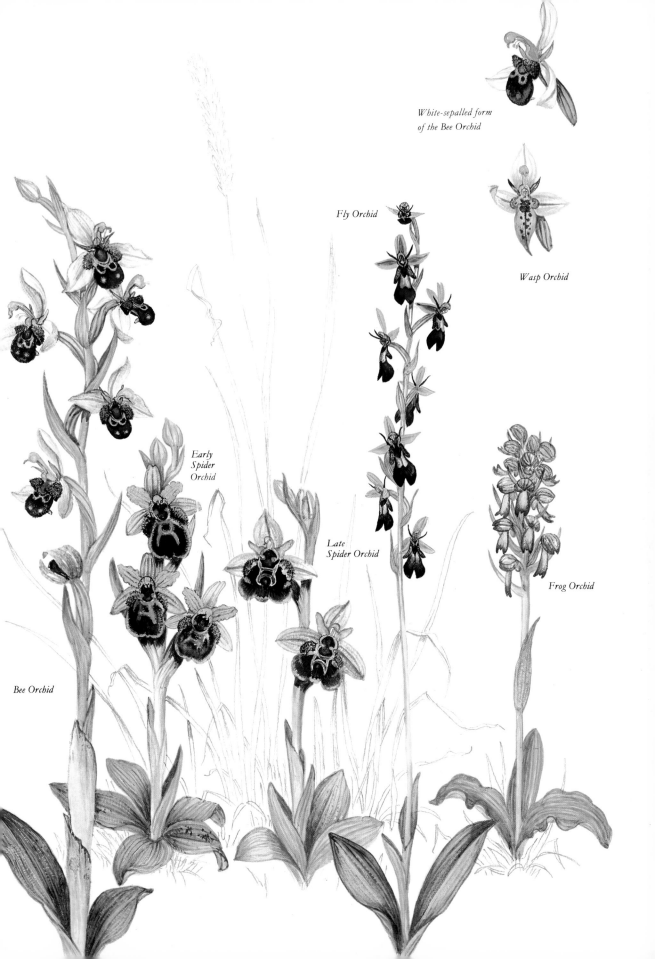

White-sepalled form of the Bee Orchid

Fly Orchid

Wasp Orchid

Early Spider Orchid

Late Spider Orchid

Frog Orchid

Bee Orchid

The **Man Orchid** (*Aceras anthropophorum*) is one of those fascinating orchids with many florets—up to ninety have been recorded—which can be found in southern Britain. The shape of the floret gives it its name since the hood is said to resemble the head and the lip the body of a person, with its four projections as the arms and legs. It grows on chalk soils in eastern England, but curiously enough it is not so confined in Continental Europe where it will grow on soil which is not particularly chalky. It flowers in May and June, dying down soon after in the open grassland and scrub in which it flourishes. The chemical coumarin is contained in its leaves which give off the pleasant scent of new-mown hay.

The distribution of the **Lizard Orchid** (*Himantoglossum hircinum*) is similar to that of the Man Orchid but it has had a varied history in Britain. The number of florets depends on the height and vigour of the plant—as many as seventy have been found but this is rare. In Britain the plant may be as small as twelve inches but on the Continent it grows to three feet. During the first thirty years of this century, the winter climate in Britain warmed very slightly with more rain coming before a less frosty spring. In the same period the Lizard Orchid extended its range considerably to the north and west, and it is reasonable to suggest that the two are linked since the improved weather pattern matches that in which the orchid grows in profusion in other countries. It is confined to calcareous soils and over limestone rocks, and we have found well-grown specimens in some of the sand dunes on the west coast of France. On one occasion we picked up a large plant which had just been cut down by a hay machine and took it to our caravan where we left it. On returning later that hot sunny day we were made aware of the reason for the species name of *hircinum*, a 'goat'. The smell of billy goat was with us for several days.

Some orchids produce a pair of large leaves before the flower stalk appears to grow up through them. The **Common Twayblade** (*Listera ovata*) has these two large ovate leaves (hence the species name) which make identification simple. Many flowers of this orchid are sterile, especially if they grow in more shady areas of woodland, requiring the plant as it matures to develop a lateral root system from which buds and later stems can grow. The flowers appear from May to July in the varying habitats which this species will tolerate. The Lesser Twayblade (*L. cordata*), whose 'face' appears on page 64 is only a third of the size of the Common species and its flowers, which appear from June to August, have a reddish tinge to them. It grows on slightly acid soils, in open meadow and wet boggy places, often hidden by heather and bracken.

The **Greater Butterfly Orchid** (*Platanthera chlorantha*) also flowers from June to August. This is a beautiful plant—tall, white and fragrant with the scent of vanilla. It has a pair of leaves at the base which, being shiny and elliptical, cannot be mistaken for those of other orchids. It grows on moors and marshy ground alongside its relative the Lesser Butterfly Orchid (*P. bifolia*). Although a stunted Greater may be smaller than a vigorous Lesser, they can still be told apart. The pollen masses in the Greater are divergent whilst in the Lesser they are parallel. This identification clue can be clearly seen on page 64. Gerard first recorded it 'growing on a heath between London and Henden, at a place called Hampstead'.

Common
Twayblade

Lizard Orchid

Orchid

Greater
Butterfly Orchid

One of the largest of our orchids is the **Lady Orchid** *(Orchis purpurea)*. It is often a robust plant, reaching a height of three feet, with large leaves and a massive spike of flowers which can itself be up to five inches long. The individual large florets are most attractive, with dark chocolate-maroon hoods and purple-spotted lips which can vary in shape. It grows in woods on chalky soil and is widespread though local in southeast Britain. It is less common than it was because of overpicking and the destruction of its habitats. In late May we like to visit these flowers in a small wood in France where they are allowed to grow to their full majestic height, unmolested and unpicked. They are a magnificent sight.

The **Burnt Orchid** *(Orchis ustulata)* is often described as the Lady Orchid in miniature. There is a similarity in the colours of the flowers, but the hood of this species is redder on the fully opened flowers and a distinctive black-maroon when in bud, this latter feature giving it its common name of Burnt Orchid and its even more descriptive one of Burnt-tip. It grows on chalk and limestone and can reach a height of eight inches in a well-grown specimen but sometimes may not exceed two inches. The sweetly scented flowers appear from mid-May onwards, if you can find them, for their colonies are decreasing and although they may appear in large numbers on a few sites they cannot be relied upon to repeat the performance every year. They require short-cropped, well-drained soil, so the undergrazing of grass by sheep and rabbits has contributed to their decline as much as the ploughing-up of old pastures.

Of the two spotted orchids, the Heath *(Dactylorhiza maculata)*, is usually found on acid or neutral soil and grows equally well in bogs or on dry moorland. The **Common Spotted Orchid** *(D. fuchsii)*, on the other hand, grows on chalky soil in marshes, light woodlands, downs and roadside verges, and is widespread throughout Britain, being fairly common in some areas. It is said to grow as tall as thirty inches, but the plant in

Lady Orchid

Burnt Orchid

our garden, which annually produces more and more flowers, does not exceed fifteen. The lowest leaf is always the smallest and most rounded, the leaves above being progressively narrower and more sharply pointed. They are usually heavily blotched and spotted although plants with plain leaves can be found.

Among our favourite orchids the **Fragrant Orchid** *(Gymnadenia conopsea)* ranks high for it is extremely dainty. The flowers are delightful, long-spurred and scented, and the plant grows to about eighteen inches tall with leaves hooded at the tip and fanning out from the lower part of the flowering stem. Once, and once only, the Short-spurred Fragrant Orchid *(G. odoratissima)* flowered in Britain, in 1922. It has never appeared again, but we live in hope that one day some Continental seed may drift down to start a new colony. It has smaller flowers, shorter spurs and narrower leaves.

An orchid rarely overlooked is the bright pink **Pyramid Orchid** *(Anacamptis pyramidalis)* which grows on chalk downland and in limestone areas, often in quite large numbers. The flower is usually distinctly pyramidal to start with, but the shape spreads out as the top flowers open. The height varies from six to eighteen inches. It may be found from June to August; the colour varies from a soft pale pink to a brilliant pure cerise.

One of the best-known orchids is the widespread and often abundant **Early Purple Orchid** *(Orchis mascula)* which flowers early in the year. It is as much at home on sea cliffs, in woodlands and on downland as in hedgerows. It can be found throughout Britain and is widespread in many other parts of the world. It has collected many local names including Long Purples in Shakespeare's time and Kettle Cases in the Isle of Wight. The upcurved spur is very characteristic and the plant is easily recognized by its usually well-spotted leaves and, in April, its magenta-purple flowers.

Fragrant Orchid

Common Spotted Orchid

Pyramid Orchid

Early Purple Orchid

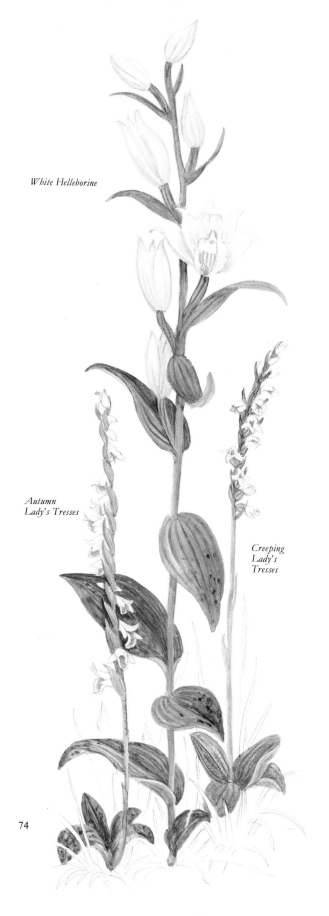

White Helleborine

Autumn
Lady's Tresses

Creeping
Lady's
Tresses

The helleborines are a slightly different group within the Orchid family and are divided into two genera—*Cephalanthera* and *Epipactis*. The former has larger and more colourful flowers, particularly the Red Helleborine *(Cephalanthera rubra)*, a beautiful and graceful plant, very rare in Britain.

The **White Helleborine** *(C. damasonium)* is the most typical beech-wood orchid and is widespread in south and east Britain, being abundant on chalky soils. It has a considerable root stock producing a mass of underground growth which can cope with dry conditions. It has greyish leaves when mature, but sometimes with a reddish tinge at first. It can carry up to sixteen flowers on each spike, but more usually half that number, and grows from six to fifteen inches tall. The flowers, which rarely fully open, are white and sometimes creamy with orange or yellow ridges of the lip, and appear in May and June.

The lady's tresses were so named by William Turner because the characteristic spiralling reminded him of the way ladies wore their hair.

The fragrant **Autumn Lady's Tresses** *(Spiranthes spiralis)* is widespread in southern Britain. A rosette of leaves grows in early autumn and overwinters, to wither and die before the flower spike blooms in August and September; sometimes the leaves of the following year's rosette grow beside the flowering stem. It is heavily dependent on fungal activity, for the buds on the spreading roots to form new colonies. The flower spike usually grows to six inches but can reach twelve, with about fifteen flowers. Summer Lady's Tresses *(S. aestivalis)* is now extinct in Britain. First recorded in 1840 in southern England where it was fairly abundant, by 1914 it had a precarious hold in the Channel Islands and was recorded in 1926 when the last colony of four plants was dug up complete with its roots. Irish Lady's Tresses *(S. romanzoffiana)* grows almost entirely in Ireland, but there

74

are a few places in the southern Outer Hebrides where it flourishes. It has a much denser flower spike with three rows of spiralling flowers.

Creeping Lady's Tresses *(Goodyera repens)* has slender creeping roots from which the stem arises. It has attractively veined leaves and a sweetly scented flower spike, three to four inches tall, whose spiral is not so well formed. Native to Scandinavia and eastern Europe, in Britain, with one exception, it grows only in Scottish pine forests. The exception is a pair of sites in a pine plantation in East Anglia where it probably arrived on the roots of transplanted trees.

The **Marsh Helleborine** *(Epipactis palustris)* is not typical of its genus. It has larger flowers of a better colour with a yellow patch at the back of the lip instead of ridges. It has a creeping habit of growth. The stem is usually twelve to eighteen inches tall with about ten florets, but larger plants have been recorded. It is widespread in Europe and in Britain away from shady places. It is pollinated by bees when it flowers from June to September.

The **Dark Red Helleborine** *(E. atrorubens)* grows on limestone rock and scree, sometimes appearing to come straight out of the rock. Its short thick roots give rise to a large amount of thin ones which spread through crevices in search of nutrition. In Britain there is usually one stem per plant but on the Continent up to six may grow, with up to twenty slightly vanilla-scented florets. It is shorter than the Broadleaved Helleborine *(E. helleborine)* for which it is occasionally mistaken, but when in flower, in June and July, the broad red sepals should clear any doubt. The attractive Violet Helleborine *(E. purpurata)* grows in woods, often beech, in clumps of purple-tinted stems around which the flowers loosely spiral. The flowers are pale green and white inside, with a mottled violet cup. It can be found mainly in southern Britain, France and Germany.

Dark Red Helleborine

Marsh Helleborine

Lady's Slipper Orchid

Ghost Orchid

Red Helleborine

Red Helleborine (*Cephalanthera rubra*) is a flower of such a pure and brilliant cerise-pink that it is not easily overlooked and has become another victim of pickers unable to resist it. It is shy of flowering in Britain and is now confined to a small area of woodland in the Cotswolds. We will always remember in a wood in France coming across a glade full of these plants, glowing pink in the sunshine. It was a sight so full of pure pleasure that it left us with feelings of regret that such a scene does not occur here.

Ghost Orchid (*Epipogium aphyllum*) is a small, pale, almost transparent yellowish plant, a mere three or four inches tall, without leaves and lacking all chlorophyll, which grows in the deep shade of beech woods and flowers only spasmodically. It sometimes stays dormant for several years until a particularly wet spring causes it to send up a flowering stem. It lives entirely on decayed matter in the soil and is found in small numbers in a few places in southeastern England. It is also found in parts of Europe and beyond, even in the Himalayas, but never in large numbers.

Lady's Slipper Orchid (*Cypripedium calceolus*), once common enough to be sold to travellers on the coach roads of northern England, has dwindled so disastrously since that it is now the rarest of Britain's rare flowers. Not so long ago, it was known to be growing in over twenty sites, but it was ruthlessly hunted by collectors obsessed by the desire to have a plant of their own. In spite of the fact that it had been known for a long time that its days would be numbered if thefts continued, one site after another was stripped of its plants, until now only one plant remains, carefully guarded by botanists who are unable to increase its numbers.

The pollen from one flower will no longer fertilize another on the same plant, and the meristem method of propagation, which works so well for most orchids, will not for the *Cypripediums*. Everything has been done that reasonably can be to discover if any of the stolen plants still survive, with no success. It is doubtful if any will now come to light, if any survive at all. The illustration for this book had to be painted from a European specimen. In outward appearance it is the same as our native one, but I felt no pleasure in drawing it, only sadness that we may never again see this species growing in Britain.

The **Military Orchid** *(Orchis militaris)* is a beautiful soft-mauve and pink orchid with dark spots. It is not uncommon in Europe—indeed we have seen long ribbons of them growing along the verges of some French lanes—but so rare in Britain that for twenty-five years it was thought to be extinct. In 1947 it was rediscovered in its old haunt in Buckinghamshire and later in a new site in East Anglia where a raised walkway has been erected to enable the public to see this almost-lost species blooming within its cage which, unlike those in zoos, is not there to prevent the wild creature from getting out, but to stop the human ones from getting in.

Monkey Orchid *(Orchis simia)* was frequently found in the Chilterns a hundred and fifty years ago when it was certainly not the rarity it is today. Its decline has been caused by the ploughing up of its chalk-down habitat and—as usual—the greed of collectors. There are now only a few well-guarded plants left, and even abroad it is sadly dwindling in numbers. It is unique among our orchids in that the top flowers of each spike usually open first.

Military Orchid

Monkey Orchid

Bearded Bellflower

Campanula cochlearifolia

Index